My KitchenAid ICE CREAM Maker Book

100 Deliciously Simple Homemade Recipes Using Your 2 Quart Stand Mixer Attachment for Frozen Fun

LILY CHARLES

KitchenAid® Ice Cream

My KitchenAid® Ice Cream Maker Book: 100 Deliciously Simple Homemade Recipes Using Your 2 Quart Stand Mixer Attachment for Frozen Fun

Copyright © 2017 Lily Charles

Cover photo credits: yuliyagontar/ Depositphotos.com

Back cover: photodesign / Depositphotos.com, Wiktory / Depositphotos.com, studioM / Depositphotos.com, keko64 / Depositphotos.com

Interior photos: All interior photos are from Depositphotos.com
Photodesign page 13, studioM page 70, Wiktory page 122, homydesign page 169, keko64 page 214

All rights reserved The use of any part of this publication reproduced, transmitted in any form or by any means, electronic, mechanical, recording or otherwise, or stored in a retrieval system, without the prior consent of the publisher is an infringement of the copyright law. In the case of photocopying or other reprographic copying of the material, a license must be obtained before proceeding.

Legal Disclaimer The information contained in this book is the opinion of the author and is based on the author's personal experience and observations. The author does not assume liability whatsoever for the use of or inability to use any or all information contained in this book, and accepts no responsibility for any loss or damages of any kind that may be incurred by the reader as a result of actions arising from the use of information in this book. Use this information at your own risk. The author reserves the right to make any changes he or she deems necessary to future versions of the publication to ensure its accuracy.

Table of contents

INTRODUCTION 8
How to Use This Book 9
Choosing a Freezing Appliance 11
Ice cream 13
    Mom's Caramel Butter Pecan Ice cream 14
    Pecan Praline Ice Cream 16
    Deep Dark Chocolate Ice Cream 18
    Perfect Pistachio Ice cream 22
    Peach Cobbler Ice Cream 24
    Va-va-voom Vanilla 26
    Chocolate Mousse Frozen Decadence 28
    Fresh Strawberry Ice Cream 30
    Chocolate Chip Cookie Dough Ice Cream 32
    Chunky Chocolate Mint 34
    Blueberry Ice Cream 36
    Cotton Candy Ice Cream 38
    Pumpkin Pie Ice Cream 40
    Cookies and Cream 42
    Peanut Butter and Bacon Ice Cream 44
    Mint Chocolate Chip 46
    Cake Batter Ice Cream 48
    Dulce de Leche Ice Cream 50
    Blackberry Chunk Ice Cream 52
    S'mores Ice cream 54

Smooth Mandarin Ice Cream 56

Rocky Road Ice cream 58

Dreamy Chocolate Ice Cream 60

Raspberry Fudge Swirl Ice Cream 62

Pineapple Upside-Down Cake Ice Cream 64

Chili Chocolate Ice Cream 66

GELATO **68**

Creamy Hibiscus Gelato 70

Classic Vanilla-Custard Gelato 72

Banana-Cream Gelato 74

Strawberry Honeysuckle Gelato 76

Salted Toffee Gelato 80

Coconut Cream Gelato 82

Peaches and Cream Gelato 86

Chocolate Cheesecake Gelato 88

Raspberry Lavender Gelato 92

Green Tea Gelato 96

Blueberry Cassis Gelato 98

Chocolate Hazelnut Gelato 102

Marvelous Mango Gelato 106

Blackberry Cream Gelato 110

Lemonade Gelato 114

Cinnamon Spice Autumn Gelato 116

Passion Fruit Nectar Gelato 118

Rosehip Tea Gelato 120

Boysenberry Cream Gelato 122

FROZEN YOGURT **126**

Pineapple Chunk Fro-Yo 128
Peanut Butter and Banana Fro-Yo 130
Watermelon Fro-Yo 132
Very Vanilla Fro-Yo 134
Orange Cream Fro-Yo 136
Minty Fresh Fro-Yo 138
Apple-Pie Fro-Yo 140
Caramel Nut Crunch Fro-Yo 142
Pear Fro-Yo 144
Triple Chocolate Fudge Brownie Fro-Yo 146
Berry Berry Fro-Yo 148
Black Forest Fro-Yo 150
Plum Cinnamon Fro-Yo 152
Raspberry Chunk Fro-Yo 154
Granola and Raisin Fro-Yo 156
Strawberry Banana Fro-Yo 158
Caramel Nougat Chocolate-Swirl Fro-Yo 160
Blueberry and White Chocolate Chip Fro-Yo 162
Guava Bliss Fro-Yo 164
Apple-Cinnamon Fro-Yo 166
Chai Tea Fro-Yo 168
Grapefruit Fro-Yo 170

SORBETS 172
Mango Lime Sorbet 174
Kiwi Citrus Sorbet 176
Orange Carrot Apple Sorbet 178
Cool and Classic Lemon Sorbet 180

Berry Blended Sorbet 182

Tropical Fandango Sorbet 184

Tarragon Sorbet 186

Black and Blueberry Sorbet 188

Cranberry Ginger Sorbet 190

Dairy Free Dark Chocolate Sorbet 192

Raspberry Mint Sorbet 194

Honeydew Melon Sorbet 196

Apple Honey Sorbet 198

All-Natural Pink Lemonade Sorbet 200

Sweet Cherry Sorbet 202

Mascarpone Sorbet 204

Peach Sorbet 206

Avocado Sorbet 208

Plum Sorbet 210

Strawberry Rhubarb Sorbet 212

Lemon Custard Sorbet 216

ADULTS ONLY 219

Irish Cream Frozen Yogurt 220

Frozen Piña Colada 222

Mocha Cream Gelato 224

Sangria Slushies 226

White Russian Gelato 228

Frozen Daiquiri 230

Italian Espresso Ice cream 232

"Old Fashioned" Vanilla Whiskey and Nuts 234

Frozen Strawberry Margarita 236

Frozen Chocolate Martini 238
Gin and Juice Fro-Yo 240
Rum Raisin Ice Cream 242
Chocolate Stout Ice Cream 244

INTRODUCTION

Most of us live relatively near the vicinity of an ice cream parlor – and also perhaps near a frozen-yogurt shop, a sorbet section in the grocery store, even a gelato stand. So I can hear you asking, *Why should I buy an at-home ice cream maker or freezing appliance when it's so easy to buy frozen sweets?*

I asked myself the same question – until a few years ago, when I helped a friend make ice cream in her kitchen with her very own ice cream maker. And then it dawned on me. When I buy ice cream (or fro-yo, sorbet, or gelato) at a café or store, I have to just accept whatever flavors they have to offer, without even really knowing what's going into the dessert in question. But with an at-home ice cream maker or freezing appliance, I can make *whatever flavors I want,* and I know exactly what ingredients are going to be enjoyed by my friends, family, and guests!

Suddenly, the possibilities seemed endless. I'd always loved my KitchenAid® stand mixer and how easy it made my job in the kitchen. So I was thrilled to find the Ice Cream Attachment designed specifically for my stand mixer. I purchased one right away and never looked back. My family has enjoyed experimenting and eating all of our different flavors and ideas. It's not only tasty, it's just plain fun for all of us!

And while I'm still serving up a decadent treat – sugar, cream, so forth – the peace of mind in knowing what ingredients I'm using is absolutely wonderful. No additives, no preservatives, none of the artificial flavors or colorings you'll find in most store-bought frozen desserts. Just wonderful flavors, and ingredients I can feel good about. It's still a "treat," but it's hard to call homemade ice cream "junk" food!

That best part of my at-home freezing appliance is, of course, the level of creativity it allows for. Baskin Robbins and its 31 flavors have nothing on me. There is really no limit to the flavors and combinations of ice creams, sorbets, frozen yogurts and gelatos one can whip up with a good freezing appliance. Your own imagination is quite literally the limit!

The recipes in this book are the result of all that experimentation. From classic flavors like vanilla and Rocky Road, to newfangled ones like my tangy kiwi-citrus sorbet, every frozen treat in here has been tested and perfected in my very own kitchen, and they've all received rave reviews from my friends, family, and guests. Quite simply, these recipes have injected some serious frozen fun into my household, and I'm confident they'll do the same at yours.

How to Use This Book

This book is organized by frozen dessert category, ice cream, gelato, frozen yogurt, and sorbet, so readers can easily find whatever type of recipe they're in the mood for. The final section, "For Adults Only," contains a mix of all those categories, plus a few more, but since they all contain either alcohol or caffeine, I put them in a separate section. Each recipe also includes a full set of instructions, so there's no need to read them in order. Skipping around to the recipe you want is fine.

Generally speaking, freezing appliances such as ice cream makers are among the more foolproof items in a kitchen. Regardless, it's important to carefully read all safety tips and product instructions that come with your freezing appliance or ice cream maker, to ensure safe and correct usage. Your appliance most likely comes with a freezer bowl in which you'll place the ingredients, and in all cases it's important not to overfill it, but instead to leave a roughly a 1-inch space at the top. Remember that ingredients tend to expand during the freezing process, so make sure to allow for that when measuring and preparing recipes.

Freezing appliances will always work best when the freezer bowl is properly frozen before incorporating the ingredients. I tend to store the freezer bowl in the freezer at all times, except when in use, so that it's always frozen and ready to go when I need it. You might find this works well for you, too. Always remember to wash and dry the freezer bowl before freezing it, and consider storing it in a plastic bag in the back of the freezer (where the temperature will be coldest) to prevent freezer burn and to keep it clean. Always keep your freezer set to 0 degrees Fahrenheit (-18 degrees Celsius).

The recipes in this book all contain preparation instructions for making sure that the bowl is properly frozen, though keep in mind that these instructions were written specifically for the KitchenAid® Ice Cream Attachment. If you're using a different appliance, even if it's similar, make sure you check the product manual and instructions extra carefully to make sure you're handling the freezer bowl and other parts correctly.

Choosing a Freezing Appliance

As a long time user of the KitchenAid® products, it was a no-brainer that my ice cream machine be compatible with my stand mixer. It's incredibly simple to use, even easier to clean and store, and sturdy as can be, just what you would expect from KitchenAid®. I've been using mine regularly for years now, and it shows virtually no sign of wear and tear, and works as wonderfully as it did the first time I used it.

KitchenAid® is a brand I've trusted my whole life for kitchen appliances, and the Ice Cream Attachment more than lives up to the high standards I've come to expect from the company. The attachment is compatible with all of the KitchenAid® stand mixers. With its help you'll be able to produce up to 2 quarts of delicious homemade ice cream, sorbet or other frozen treats.

Your KitchenAid® Ice Cream Attachment will come with the ice cream freezer bowl, a spring loaded assembly drive, a converter ring for select models and a dasher to mix the ice cream.

Set up is quite simple. First attach the assembly drive to the bottom of the mixer head. Use side A if you have a tilt head model and side B if you have the bowl lift model. The dasher will fit into the assembly drive and sit inside the freezer bowl. The freezer bowl rests on the clamping plate and locks in by turning counterclockwise. You are now ready to make ice cream!

The freezer bowl is a double walled bowl with liquid in the middle. This design keeps the blending ice cream cold and allows for uniform freezing to take place. Make sure to keep the freezer bowl in the freezer with the temperature set to at least 0 degrees Fahrenheit for at least 15 hours before the attachment is used.

When your ice cream adventure is complete, use a rubber spatula to scrape out any ice cream from the freezer bowl. A rubber spatula will prevent any damage to the inside of the bowl. Also be sure to fully thaw before washing to prevent any cracking to the freezer bowl. When thawed, it can be washed with warm soapy water. The dasher and the assembly drive are both dish washer safe.

As you can see, KitchenAid® has thought of everything to make home freezing as simple and enjoyable as possible. And now, without any further delay, read on to get the absolute best of my recipes for home-made ice cream, gelato, frozen yogurt, sorbet, and adults only treats! I hope you have as much fun with these recipes and your freezing appliance as I've had with mine.

ICE CREAM

Ok, let's be honest, when someone says the words "home freezing appliance," the first thing that comes to mind is an ice cream parlor right in one's very own kitchen...yes? Well, that's definitely true in my case. And even now, after I've been making my own ice cream at home for years, the childlike joy at doing it all by myself in my own kitchen, with any flavors my heart desires, has not warn off.

This section is my celebration of that childlike joy and of all the luscious flavors that only high-quality homemade ice cream can inspire. Of course I've included the recipes for everyone's favorite classics, strawberry, butter-pecan, cookies and cream... These are requisite in any well-stocked freezer, and my dessert menu would be nothing without them.

This section is also chock-full of some of my more inventive creations (only the experiments that succeeded, I promise) – like cotton candy ice cream, which is a much requested favorite in my household. Or how about some pumpkin pie ice cream, with a crumbled graham-cracker crust? Or perhaps some creamy vanilla with fresh blueberries swirled and chunked throughout in all their frozen juicy goodness? Or – well, I could go on, but there's ice cream to be made! Have fun with these recipes, traditional and whimsical alike, and serve with a smile.

Mom's Caramel Butter Pecan Ice cream

This recipe comes to me from my mother, who loves butter pecan ice cream more than anyone I know. For as long as I've known her, (which is my whole life) she has indulged in one single, solitary bite of butter pecan ice cream (homemade or store bought from wherever – as long as it's "butter pecan") every single night before bed, without fail. And just the one bite – don't ask me how she does it! Just enjoy this recipe from a true connoisseur.

INGREDIENTS:

1 cup of soft caramel, homemade or store bought (any brand will do)

4 tablespoons of unsalted butter

4 tablespoons of coarsely chopped pecans

1 teaspoon of kosher salt

1 1/8 cups of white sugar

1 ½ cups of whole milk

3 cups of heavy cream

2 teaspoons of pure vanilla extract

INSTRUCTIONS:

1. Make sure your freezer is set at or below 0 degrees Fahrenheit (-18 degrees Celsius). Place the ice cream bowl attachment in the freezer for at least 15 hours.

2. Check that the ice cream bowl is completely frozen by giving it a shake before use. If you hear no movement, the bowl's cooling liquid is properly frozen.

3. In a large skillet, melt the butter and add in the chopped pecans and kosher salt. Stir continuously and cook on a medium to low heat until the pecans are toasted and fragrant – about 4-5 minutes.

4. Remove from heat and strain (the butter will have a pecan flavor and can be conserved for a different use) the nuts, then cover and chill in the refrigerator.

5. In the still warm and buttery skillet, place the caramel pieces to soften on a *very* low heat. After a few minutes, the caramel will melt to a semi liquid texture, but be careful not to let it burn or stick to the skillet!

6. Using your stand mixer and a mixing bowl, while the caramel is softening, blend the milk and sugar. Stir until the sugar is fully dissolved.

7. Add in the heavy cream, vanilla extract and stir until all ingredients are evenly combined.

8. Drizzle and fold in the warm caramel directly from the skillet with just two or three strokes of a wooden spoon. Do not attempt to fully mix in the caramel, just distribute swirls of it throughout the mixture. Place the bowl in the refrigerator for 1-2 hours.

9. Take the ice cream freezer bowl out of the freezer and set it on the middle of your stand mixer's base.

10. Slide the assembly drive onto the bottom of the mixer head. Fit the dasher into the bowl and connect to the assembly drive.

11. When your stand mixer is prepared, switch it into "Level 1" or "Stir" mode. The dasher will begin to turn in the bowl. Pour the refrigerated mixture immediately from the mixing bowl into the freezer bowl.

12. After approximately 20 minutes (in the last five minutes of freezing), add the chilled toasted pecans into the ice cream bowl to let mix completely.

13. After approximately 25-30 minutes (total), the mixture will have frozen to a thick, creamy soft-serve consistency.

PECAN PRALINE ICE CREAM

Pralines are a traditional southern candy featuring pecans in a caramelized coating. They are delicious, so its only natural to to make it into a frozen confection. You could even double the batch of praline you make to use as an ice cream topping or special treat.

INGREDIENTS:

2 cups of whole milk

5 egg yolks

2 cups sugar, divided

4 tablespoons butter

¼ teaspoon sea salt

1 cup half and half

1 teaspoon vanilla extract

¼ cup pecans, chopped

INSTRUCTIONS:

1. Make sure your freezer is set at or below 0 degrees Fahrenheit (-18 degrees Celsius). Place the ice cream bowl attachment in the freezer for at least 15 hours.

2. Check that the ice cream bowl is completely frozen by giving it a shake before use. If you hear no movement, the bowl's cooling liquid is properly frozen.

3. In a medium saucepan, spread 1 ½ cups sugar and warm over medium high heat. When the sides begin to melt, stir so the sugar will begin to caramelize. When fully caramelized, remove from heat and mix in the butter and salt.

4. When butter is melted, stir in the half and half. If the mixture starts to harden, place over very low heat and stir, until it is soft again. Stir in 1 cup whole milk.

5. Using your stand mixer and a mixing bowl, beat the egg yolks. Stir in 1 cup of the caramel sauce and mix well.

6. Add the egg mixture to the saucepan with the caramel sauce and continue to stir constantly over medium heat until the mixture has thickened to a custard consistency.

7. Remove the saucepan from the heat. Add in 1 cup whole milk and vanilla extract. Stir thoroughly until evenly combined.

8. Cool and then cover and refrigerate for at least 6 hours, until completely chilled.

9. Add wax paper to a small baking sheet. To make pralines, add ½ cup of sugar to a small saucepan and place over medium heat. When edged begin to melt, stir until caramelized.

10. Remove from the heat source and stir in the chopped pecans. Pour over the prepared baking sheet. Tilt sheet to allow caramel to spread into a thin layer. It will harden as it sits. When completely hardened, use a hammer or mallet to crush into tiny, bite sized bits.

11. Take the ice cream freezer bowl out of the freezer and set it on the middle of your stand mixer's base. Slide the assembly drive onto the bottom of the mixer head. Fit the dasher into the bowl and connect to the assembly drive.

12. When your stand mixer is prepared, switch it into "Level 1" or "Stir" mode. The dasher will begin to turn in the bowl. Pour the refrigerated custard mixture immediately from the mixing bowl into the freezer bowl.

13. After approximately 20 minutes (in the last five minutes of freezing), add the crushed pralines into the freezer bowl to let mix completely.

14. After approximately 30 minutes, the mixture will have frozen to a dense, creamy soft-serve consistency laced with sweet pralines.

KitchenAid® Ice Cream

Too rich

✓ DEEP DARK CHOCOLATE ICE CREAM

For those who like their chocolate ice cream deep, dark, and rich as can be, this is the recipe for you. The custard like consistency of the base ensures that every spoonful of this ice cream is pure dense decadence. I particularly love the intensity of the Dutch cocoa in addition to the bittersweet chocolate. This ice cream is for serious chocolate lovers, so get ready to fall in love!

INGREDIENTS:

2 ¼ cups of whole milk

2 ¼ cup of heavy cream

1 whole vanilla bean

1 1/8 cups of white sugar

1 1/8 cups of Dutch process chocolate cocoa

2 large eggs, whole

2 large egg yolks (separated from the whites)

12 ounces of coarsely chopped bittersweet chocolate

2 teaspoons of pure vanilla extract

INSTRUCTIONS:

1. Make sure your freezer is set at or below 0 degrees Fahrenheit (-18 degrees Celsius). Place the ice cream bowl attachment in the freezer for at least 15 hours.

2. Check that the ice cream bowl is completely frozen by giving it a shake before use. If you hear no movement, the bowl's cooling liquid is properly frozen.

3. In a large saucepan, mix the whole milk and the heavy cream over a medium to low heat.

4. Using a sharp knife, split the vanilla bean down the middle lengthwise, then use the blunt end of the knife to scrape out the seeds of the bean.

5. Stir the seeds and the bean pod into the heating milk and cream mixture in the saucepan, and simmer on a low heat for approximately 30 minutes.

6. Extract the vanilla bean pod and discard it, and reduce the heat under the saucepan to the lowest setting.

7. Using your stand mixer and a mixing bowl, beat or whisk the sugar, Dutch process cocoa, whole eggs and egg yolks, and continue to beat or whisk until the mixture has thickened to a mayonnaise-like consistency.

8. Reduce the speed of the mixer to a low speed, and add in one cup of the hot milk and cream mixture to the mixing bowl. Mix until evenly and smoothly blended.

9. Stir the chopped bittersweet chocolate into the remaining milk and cream mixture in the saucepan, and stir continuously with a wooden spoon until the chocolate is melted and evenly blended in with the milk and cream mixture.

10. Add the egg mixture, and continue to stir constantly over low heat, until the mixture has thickened to a chocolate pudding like consistency.

11. Remove the saucepan from the heat and transfer the mixture to a large mixing bowl. Add in the vanilla extract and stir thoroughly until evenly combined.

12. Cover and refrigerate for at least 2 hours, until completely cooled.

13. Take the ice cream freezer bowl out of the freezer and set it on the middle of your stand mixer's base. Slide the assembly drive onto the bottom of the mixer head. Fit the dasher into the bowl and connect to the assembly drive.

KitchenAid® Ice Cream

14. When your stand mixer is prepared, switch it into "Level 1" or "Stir" mode. The dasher will begin to turn in the bowl. Pour the refrigerated mixture immediately from the mixing bowl into the freezer bowl.

15. After approximately 30 minutes, the mixture will have frozen to a dense, creamy soft-serve consistency. Serve directly from the ice cream freezer bowl into serving bowls or cones, and enjoy!

16. For a more hard-frozen consistency, transfer the mixture from the freezer bowl into an air-tight container and keep in the freezer for at least 2 more hours.

LILY CHARLES

PERFECT PISTACHIO ICE CREAM

There is something about the flavor of a pistachio nut that is absolutely irresistible to me. I'm one of those people who could eat a whole bagful of pistachio nuts – or, better yet, scoop after scoop of my own homemade pistachio ice cream. If I do say so myself, pistachios don't get any better than this, frozen and infused through perfectly luscious ice cream.

INGREDIENTS:

1/3 cups of whole milk, chilled

1 1/8 cups of granulated sugar

3 cups of heavy cream, chilled

1 teaspoon of pure almond extract

1 ½ teaspoons of pure vanilla extract

1 ½ cup of lightly salted or unsalted shelled green pistachio nuts, coarsely chopped

INSTRUCTIONS:

17. Make sure your freezer is set at or below 0 degrees Fahrenheit (-18 degrees Celsius). Place the ice cream bowl attachment in the freezer for at least 15 hours.
18. Check that the ice cream bowl is completely frozen by giving it a shake before use. If you hear no movement, the bowl's cooling liquid is properly frozen.

19. Using your stand mixer and a mixing bowl, combine the milk and sugar, at a low speed until the sugar is fully dissolved in the milk, for approximately 1-2 minutes.
20. Stir in the heavy cream, the almond and the vanilla extracts, and stir thoroughly until all ingredients are evenly blended. Refrigerate mixture for 1-2 hours.
21. Take the ice cream freezer bowl out of the freezer and set it on the middle of your stand mixer's base.
22. Slide the assembly drive onto the bottom of the mixer head. Fit the dasher into the bowl and connect to the assembly drive.
23. When your stand mixer is prepared, switch it into "Level 1" or "Stir" mode. The dasher will begin to turn in the bowl. Pour the refrigerated mixture immediately from the mixing bowl into the freezer bowl.
24. After approximately 20 minutes (in the last five minutes of freezing), add the coarsely chopped pistachio nuts into the ice cream bowl to let mix completely.
25. After approximately 25-30 minutes (total), the mixture will have frozen to a thick, creamy soft-serve consistency, with the frozen pistachio chunks perfectly blended throughout. Serve directly from the ice cream freezer bowl into serving bowls or cones, and enjoy!
26. For a more hard-frozen consistency, transfer the mixture from the freezer bowl into an air-tight container and keep in the freezer for at least 2 more hours.

PEACH COBBLER ICE CREAM

I have a serious weakness for peach cobbler. The perfect summer dessert flavors, lightly spiced and sweet as can be, tucked into the ultimate crispy delicious comfort food that is the cobbler format makes it hard to resist This ice cream blend is inspired by that beloved dessert, marrying luscious ice cream with those classic peach-cobbler flavors and textures. I can't get enough of this one, and trust you'll love it as much as I do! Serve with a dollop of whipped cream and an extra sprinkle of brown sugar on top.

INGREDIENTS:

1 ½ cups of whole milk

1 cup of packed brown sugar

1 tablespoon of molasses

2 cups of peaches (fresh and peeled, or canned and drained), cut into small bite-sized pieces

¾ teaspoon of powdered cinnamon

¾ teaspoon of ground nutmeg

2 ½ cups of heavy cream

1 teaspoon of pure vanilla extract

1 cup of crumbled gingersnaps or graham crackers

INSTRUCTIONS:

1. Make sure your freezer is set at or below 0 degrees Fahrenheit (-18 degrees Celsius). Place the ice cream bowl attachment in the freezer for at least 15 hours.

2. Check that the ice cream bowl is completely frozen by giving it a shake before use. If you hear no movement, the bowl's cooling liquid is properly frozen.

3. Using your stand mixer and a mixing bowl, combine the milk, brown sugar and molasses at a low speed until the sugar is fully dissolved.

4. Stir in the cinnamon, nutmeg, heavy cream, and vanilla. Stir thoroughly until all ingredients are evenly blended. Place the mixture in the refrigerator for 2 hours.

5. Take the ice cream freezer bowl out of the freezer and set it on the middle of your stand mixer's base.

6. Slide the assembly drive onto the bottom of the mixer head. Fit the dasher into the bowl and connect to the assembly drive.

7. When your stand mixer is prepared, switch it into "Level 1" or "Stir" mode. The dasher will begin to turn in the bowl. Pour the refrigerated mixture immediately from the mixing bowl into the freezer bowl.

8. After approximately 20 minutes (in the last five minutes of freezing), add the peach chunks and crumbled graham crackers or gingersnaps into the freezer bowl to let mix completely.

9. After approximately 25-30 minutes (total), the mixture will have frozen to a thick, creamy soft-serve consistency, with the crumbled cookies and peaches perfectly frozen and embedded throughout. Serve directly from the ice cream freezer bowl into bowls or cones, and enjoy!

10. For a more hard-frozen consistency, transfer the mixture from the freezer bowl into an air-tight container and keep in the freezer for at least 2 more hours.

Va-va-voom Vanilla

I have to scoff (internally) every time I hear someone use the word "vanilla" as colloquial shorthand for something boring, mundane, or dull, because that person has clearly never tried my homemade vanilla-bean ice cream. This recipe makes a luscious, velvety-smooth and oh, so sweet ice cream, which everyone can get excited about. Try this recipe and I promise, you'll never think of vanilla as boring again.

INGREDIENTS:

1 ½ cups of whole milk

1 ¼ cups of granulated sugar

3 cups of heavy cream

1 tablespoon of pure vanilla extract

1 teaspoon of coarsely ground vanilla bean

INSTRUCTIONS:

1. Make sure your freezer is set at or below 0 degrees Fahrenheit (-18 degrees Celsius). Place the ice cream bowl attachment in the freezer for at least 15 hours.

2. Check that the ice cream bowl is completely frozen by giving it a shake before use. If you hear no movement, the bowl's cooling liquid is properly frozen.

3. Using your stand mixer and a mixing bowl, combine the milk and sugar at a low speed until the sugar is fully dissolved in the milk.

4. Stir in the vanilla extract, vanilla bean, and the heavy cream. Stir thoroughly until all ingredients are evenly blended. Place the mixture in the refrigerator for 2 hours.

5. Take the ice cream freezer bowl out of the freezer and set it on the middle of your stand mixer's base.
6. Slide the assembly drive onto the bottom of the mixer head. Fit the dasher into the bowl and connect to the assembly drive.
7. When your stand mixer is prepared, switch it into "Level 1" or "Stir" mode. The dasher will begin to turn in the bowl. Pour the refrigerated mixture immediately from the mixing bowl into the freezer bowl.
8. After approximately 25-30 minutes, the mixture will have frozen to a thick, creamy soft-serve consistency. Serve directly from the ice cream freezer bowl into serving bowls or cones, and enjoy!
9. For a more hard-frozen consistency, transfer the mixture from the freezer bowl into an air-tight container and keep in the freezer for at least 2 more hours.

Chocolate Mousse Frozen Decadence

Is there anything better than good chocolate mousse - rich dark cocoa, lightly sweetened with white and brown sugar, with just enough cream to make every bite smooth, fluffy and luscious? Actually, I can think of one thing - that exact same treat, in frozen ice cream form. Look no further than this awesome recipe for chocolate mousse ice cream. My family and friends all love it, and I know yours will, too.

INGREDIENTS:

1 cup of unsweetened dark cocoa powder

2/3 cup of white sugar

½ cup of packed brown sugar

1 ½ cups of whole milk

3 ¼ cups of heavy cream

1 tablespoon of pure vanilla extract

INSTRUCTIONS:

1. Make sure your freezer is set at or below 0 degrees Fahrenheit (-18 degrees Celsius). Place the ice cream bowl attachment in the freezer for at least 15 hours.

2. Check that the ice cream bowl is completely frozen by giving it a shake before use. If you hear no movement, the bowl's cooling liquid is properly frozen.

3. Using your stand mixer and a mixing bowl, combine the cocoa, brown and white sugar, and stir until evenly combined.

4. Add the whole milk and combine until the cocoa and sugars are fully dissolved in the milk.

5. Stir in the vanilla extract and the heavy cream. Stir thoroughly until all ingredients are evenly blended. Place the mixture in the refrigerator for 2 hours.

6. Take the ice cream freezer bowl out of the freezer and set it on the middle of your stand mixer's base.

7. Slide the assembly drive onto the bottom of the mixer head. Fit the dasher into the bowl and connect to the assembly drive.

8. When your stand mixer is prepared, switch it into "Level 1" or "Stir" mode. The dasher will begin to turn in the bowl. Pour the refrigerated mixture immediately from the mixing bowl into the freezer bowl.

9. After approximately 25-30 minutes, the mixture will have frozen to a thick, creamy soft-serve consistency. Serve directly from the ice cream freezer bowl into serving bowls or cones, and enjoy!

10. For a more hard-frozen consistency, transfer the mixture from the freezer bowl into an air-tight container and keep in the freezer for at least 2 more hours.

FRESH STRAWBERRY ICE CREAM

This flavor is a classic for good reason. The combination of fresh strawberries and cold frozen cream is pure bliss, and a wonderful accompaniment to any number of desserts or a serious treat all on its own. This ice cream is one that I like to keep handy in my freezer at any given time, if I've got the space in my icebox. I never need a reason to whip up a fresh batch because it goes fast!

INGREDIENTS:

3 cups of fresh ripe strawberries, rinsed and patted dry, sliced with the stems removed

4 tablespoons of freshly squeezed lemon juice

1 ½ cups of white sugar

1 ½ cups of whole milk

2 ¾ cups of heavy cream

1 ½ teaspoons of pure vanilla extract

INSTRUCTIONS:

1. Make sure your freezer is set at or below 0 degrees Fahrenheit (-18 degrees Celsius). Place the ice cream bowl attachment in the freezer for at least 15 hours.

2. Check that the ice cream bowl is completely frozen by giving it a shake before use. If you hear no movement, the bowl's cooling liquid is properly frozen.

3. Using your stand mixer and a mixing bowl, stir the sliced strawberries, the lemon juice, and ½ cup of the sugar.

4. Stir until strawberries are fully coated and the lemon juice and sugar are evenly blended, then leave to sit so that the strawberries can soak up the lemon and sugar for approximately two hours.

5. Strain the berries in a fine mesh sieve and conserve the juice.

6. Using a hand-masher, food processor or blender, mash or puree half of the berries until quite smooth.

7. Using your stand mixer and a mixing bowl, stir the milk with the remaining sugar until the sugar is fully dissolved.

8. Stir in the vanilla extract, the heavy cream, the reserved berry juice and the mashed berries, stirring thoroughly until all ingredients are evenly combined. Place the mixture in the refrigerator for 2 hours.

9. Take the ice cream freezer bowl out of the freezer and set it on the middle of your stand mixer's base.

10. Slide the assembly drive onto the bottom of the mixer head. Fit the dasher into the bowl and connect to the assembly drive.

11. When your stand mixer is prepared, switch it into "Level 1" or "Stir" mode. The dasher will begin to turn in the bowl. Pour the refrigerated mixture immediately from the mixing bowl into the freezer bowl.

12. After approximately 20 minutes (in the last five minutes of freezing), add the reserved sliced and strained strawberries into the ice cream bowl to let mix completely.

13. After approximately 25-30 minutes (total), the mixture will have frozen to a thick, creamy soft-serve consistency, with the frozen berry slices packed with juicy goodness. Serve directly from the ice cream freezer bowl into serving bowls or cones, and enjoy!

14. For a more hard-frozen consistency, transfer the mixture from the freezer bowl into an air-tight container and keep in the freezer for at least 2 more hours.

Chocolate Chip Cookie Dough Ice Cream

This chunky cookie dough ice cream is an old favorite and it's not hard to see why. I generally use Pillsbury's frozen cookie dough in my preparation, since it's usually the easiest option, though any homemade or store bought cookie dough will do as long as the dough is fully chilled ahead of time. This ice cream is a serious treat for kids and adults alike. My whole family loves it, and I know yours will too.

INGREDIENTS:

1 ½ cups of completely chilled chocolate chip cookie dough, crumbled or cut into bite-sized chunks

1 ½ cups of white sugar

1 ½ cups of whole milk

2 ¾ cups of heavy cream

2 teaspoons of pure vanilla extract

INSTRUCTIONS:

1. Make sure your freezer is set at or below 0 degrees Fahrenheit (-18 degrees Celsius). Place the ice cream bowl attachment in the freezer for at least 15 hours.

2. Check that the ice cream bowl is completely frozen by giving it a shake before use. If you hear no movement, the bowl's cooling liquid is properly frozen.

3. Using your stand mixer and a mixing bowl, stir the milk with the sugar until the sugar is fully dissolved.

4. Stir in the vanilla extract and the heavy cream, stirring thoroughly until all ingredients are evenly combined. Place the bowl in the refrigerator to chill for 1-2 hours.

5. Take the ice cream freezer bowl out of the freezer and set it on the middle of your stand mixer's base.

6. Slide the assembly drive onto the bottom of the mixer head. Fit the dasher into the bowl and connect to the assembly drive.

7. When your stand mixer is prepared, switch it into "Level 1" or "Stir" mode. The dasher will begin to turn in the bowl. Pour the refrigerated mixture immediately from the mixing bowl into the freezer bowl.

8. After approximately 20 minutes (in the last five minutes of freezing), add the chilled chunks of cookie dough into the ice cream bowl to let mix completely.

9. After approximately 25-30 minutes (total), the mixture will have frozen to a thick, creamy soft-serve consistency, with the frozen cookie dough packed into every bite. Serve directly from the ice cream freezer bowl into serving bowls or cones, and enjoy!

10. For a more hard-frozen consistency, transfer the mixture from the freezer bowl into an air-tight container and keep in the freezer for at least 2 more hours.

Chunky Chocolate Mint

Seeing as I put my mother's favorite ice cream in this book, I'd be remiss if I didn't also include my Dad's favorite. This is a creation of my mother's, after she found my father emptying entire packets of Peppermint Patty mint candies onto his ice cream as a makeshift topping. My mother took that idea and finessed it into this fantastic recipe that my whole family loves. I hope yours will too!

INGREDIENTS:

¾ cup of chocolate syrup

3 tablespoons of granulated sugar

1 ½ cups of whole milk

3 cups of heavy cream

1 teaspoon of peppermint extract

1 cup of chopped chocolate mint candies or mint chocolate morsels (I use chopped "Peppermint Patty" candies. Any homemade or store bought mint chocolate candies would do).

INSTRUCTIONS:

1. Make sure your freezer is set at or below 0 degrees Fahrenheit (-18 degrees Celsius). Place the ice cream bowl attachment in the freezer for at least 15 hours.

2. Check that the ice cream bowl is completely frozen by giving it a shake before use. If you hear no movement, the bowl's cooling liquid is properly frozen.

3. Using your stand mixer and a mixing bowl, blend the milk, chocolate syrup, and sugar. Stir until the sugar is fully dissolved.

4. Add in the heavy cream and peppermint extract, and stir until all ingredients are evenly combined. Place the mixture in the refrigerator for 1-2 hours.
5. Take the ice cream freezer bowl out of the freezer and set it on the middle of your stand mixer's base.
6. Slide the assembly drive onto the bottom of the mixer head. Fit the dasher into the bowl and connect to the assembly drive.
7. When your stand mixer is prepared, switch it into "Level 1" or "Stir" mode. The dasher will begin to turn in the bowl. Pour the refrigerated mixture immediately from the mixing bowl into the freezer bowl.
8. After approximately 20 minutes (in the last five minutes of freezing), add the chopped mint chocolate candies into the freezer bowl to let mix completely.
9. After approximately 25-30 minutes (total), the mixture will have frozen to a thick, creamy soft-serve consistency, laden with perfect melt in your mouth frozen mint chocolate candies. Serve directly from the ice cream freezer bowl into bowls or cones, and enjoy!
10. For a more hard-frozen consistency, transfer the mixture from the freezer bowl into an air-tight container and keep in the freezer for at least 2 more hours.

BLUEBERRY ICE CREAM

In the heat of the summer, when the blueberries are ripe and plentiful, this is the perfect ice cream to serve to your family. It is bursting with flavor and gorgeous in color. If blueberries are not in season, you can use frozen fruit, making this a flavor you can enjoy year round.

INGREDIENTS:

2 cups blueberries

1 cup of sugar, divided

1 tablespoon lemon juice

2 cups heavy cream

1 cup of whole milk

½ teaspoon of vanilla extract

¼ teaspoon salt

3 egg yolks

INSTRUCTIONS:

1. Make sure your freezer is set at or below 0 degrees Fahrenheit (-18 degrees Celsius). Place the ice cream bowl attachment in the freezer for at least 15 hours.

2. Check that the ice cream bowl is completely frozen by giving it a shake before use. If you hear no movement, the bowl's cooling liquid is properly frozen.

3. In a small saucepan, combine the blueberries with the lemon juice and ¼ cup of sugar. Bring to a boil over medium heat and mash the berries when they are soft. Pour through a fine mesh strainer and set the puree aside. Discard any skins or seeds.

4. In a saucepan of at least 2 ½ quarts capacity, bring the sugar, 1 cup of the half and half, milk and salt to simmer over a medium heat. Stir continuously and, once the sugar is fully dissolved, adjust the heat to low to keep the mixture warm.

5. Using your stand mixer and a mixing bowl, beat or whisk the egg yolks.

6. Reduce the speed of the mixer to a low speed, and add in one cup of the hot milk and cream mixture to the mixing bowl. Mix until evenly and smoothly blended.

7. Pour egg mixture into the saucepan with the warm cream and milk and thoroughly stir together. Add and mix in the blueberry puree.

8. Raise the heat under the saucepan to medium. Stir the mixture continuously with a wooden spoon, until the mixture has reached a custard-like consistency. Strain the custard from the saucepan into a medium sized bowl with a fine mesh strainer.

9. Add in the remaining heavy cream and vanilla extract. Bring the custard to room temperature and then cover and refrigerate for at least 1-2 hours.

10. Take the ice cream freezer bowl out of the freezer and set it on the middle of your stand mixer's base. Slide the assembly drive onto the bottom of the mixer head. Fit the dasher into the bowl and connect to the assembly drive.

11. When your stand mixer is prepared, switch it into "Level 1" or "Stir" mode. The dasher will begin to turn in the bowl. Pour the refrigerated mixture immediately from the mixing bowl into the freezer bowl.

12. After approximately 25-30 minutes, the mixture will have frozen to a dense, creamy soft-serve consistency. Serve directly from the ice cream freezer bowl into serving bowls or cones, and enjoy!

13. For a more hard-frozen consistency, transfer the mixture from the freezer bowl into an air-tight container and keep in the freezer for at least 2 more hours.

COTTON CANDY ICE CREAM

This is the perfect ice cream to serve to the kiddos, or the kid in you! Its the perfect ice cream for a birthday party because of its fun coloring and carnival-like flavor. Cotton candy syrup can easily be found online or in some specialty party stores.

INGREDIENTS:

¾ cup sugar

1 cup whole milk

2 cups of heavy cream

½ cup cotton candy syrup

1 teaspoon vanilla extract

food coloring (optional)

INSTRUCTIONS:

1. Make sure your freezer is set at or below 0 degrees Fahrenheit (-18 degrees Celsius). Place the ice cream bowl attachment in the freezer for at least 15 hours.

2. Check that the ice cream bowl is completely frozen by giving it a shake before use. If you hear no movement, the bowl's cooling liquid is properly frozen.

3. Using your stand mixer and a mixing bowl, combine the milk and sugar at a low speed until the sugar is fully dissolved in the milk.

4. Stir in the vanilla extract, heavy cream and the cotton candy syrup. Stir thoroughly until all ingredients are evenly blended.

5. Add food coloring if you are going to use it. Start with just a few drops and add until desired color is achieved. Place the mixture in the refrigerator for 2 hours.

6. Take the ice cream freezer bowl out of the freezer and set it on the middle of your stand mixer's base.

7. Slide the assembly drive onto the bottom of the mixer head. Fit the dasher into the bowl and connect to the assembly drive.

8. When your stand mixer is prepared, switch it into "Level 1" or "Stir" mode. The dasher will begin to turn in the bowl. Pour the refrigerated mixture immediately from the mixing bowl into the freezer bowl.

9. After approximately 25-30 minutes, the mixture will have frozen to a thick, creamy soft-serve consistency. Serve directly from the ice cream freezer bowl into serving bowls or cones, and enjoy!

10. For a more hard-frozen consistency, transfer the mixture from the freezer bowl into an air-tight container and keep in the freezer for at least 2 more hours.

PUMPKIN PIE ICE CREAM

This blend is a seasonal favorite at my house, though I daresay I never get sick of it and often find myself hankering for this pumpkin spiced frozen goodness in the middle of summer, too. If you're looking for a fun and delicious twist on those classic pumpkin pie flavors, look no further than this awesome ice cream. Serve with plenty of whipped cream, just as you would the pie!

INGREDIENTS:

1 ½ cups of whole milk

1 cup of packed brown sugar

2 tablespoons of molasses

1 ¾ cups of solid-packed pumpkin puree (any brand or preparation will do)

1 ½ teaspoons of powdered cinnamon

1 teaspoon of ground ginger

¼ teaspoon of ground nutmeg

2 ½ cups of heavy cream

1 teaspoon of pure vanilla extract

1 cup of crumbled gingersnaps or graham crackers

INSTRUCTIONS:

1. Make sure your freezer is set at or below 0 degrees Fahrenheit (-18 degrees Celsius). Place the ice cream bowl attachment in the freezer for at least 15 hours.

2. Check that the ice cream bowl is completely frozen by giving it a shake before use. If you hear no movement, the bowl's cooling liquid is properly frozen.

3. Using your stand mixer and a mixing bowl, combine the milk, brown sugar and molasses until the sugar is fully dissolved.

4. Stir in the pumpkin puree, cinnamon, ginger, nutmeg, heavy cream, and vanilla. Stir thoroughly until all ingredients are evenly blended. Then refrigerate for 1-2 hours.

5. Take the ice cream freezer bowl out of the freezer and set it on the middle of your stand mixer's base.

6. Slide the assembly drive onto the bottom of the mixer head. Fit the dasher into the bowl and connect to the assembly drive.

7. When your stand mixer is prepared, switch it into "Level 1" or "Stir" mode. The dasher will begin to turn in the bowl. Pour the refrigerated mixture immediately from the mixing bowl into the freezer bowl.

8. After approximately 20 minutes (in the last five minutes of freezing), add the crumbled graham crackers or gingersnaps into the freezer bowl to let mix completely.

9. After approximately 25-30 minutes (total), the mixture will have frozen to a thick, creamy soft-serve consistency, with the crumbled cookies perfectly frozen and embedded throughout. Serve directly from the ice cream freezer bowl into bowls or cones, and enjoy!

10. For a more hard-frozen consistency, transfer the mixture from the freezer bowl into an air-tight container and keep in the freezer for at least 2 more hours.

COOKIES AND CREAM

Here's another classic ice cream parlor flavor that is even more fun and delicious to make at home. The traditional preparation calls for crumbled Oreo cookies. That is typically how I make it in my home, though by all means, feel free to substitute for any other cookie (Nutter Butters also work particularly well).

INGREDIENTS:

2 cups of cooled cookies (Oreos, Nutter-Butters, or any other homemade or store bought cookie of the chef's choice), crumbled into bite-sized chunks

1 ½ cups of white sugar

1 ½ cups of whole milk

2 ¾ cups of heavy cream

2 teaspoons of pure vanilla extract

INSTRUCTIONS:

1. Make sure your freezer is set at or below 0 degrees Fahrenheit (-18 degrees Celsius). Place the ice cream bowl attachment in the freezer for at least 15 hours.
2. Check that the ice cream bowl is completely frozen by giving it a shake before use. If you hear no movement, the bowl's cooling liquid is properly frozen.
3. Using your stand mixer and a mixing bowl, stir the milk with the sugar until the sugar is fully dissolved.
4. Stir in the vanilla extract and the heavy cream, stirring thoroughly until all ingredients are evenly combined. Chill in the refrigerator for 1-2 hours.

5. Take the ice cream freezer bowl out of the freezer and set it on the middle of your stand mixer's base.

6. Slide the assembly drive onto the bottom of the mixer head. Fit the dasher into the bowl and connect to the assembly drive.

7. When your stand mixer is prepared, switch it into "Level 1" or "Stir" mode. The dasher will begin to turn in the bowl. Pour the refrigerated mixture immediately from the mixing bowl into the freezer bowl.

8. After approximately 20 minutes (in the last five minutes of freezing), add the crumbled cookie chunks into the ice cream bowl to let mix completely.

9. After approximately 25-30 minutes (total), the mixture will have frozen to a thick, creamy soft-serve consistency, with the crumbled cookies evenly distributed throughout. Serve directly from the ice cream freezer bowl into serving bowls or cones, and enjoy!

10. For a more hard-frozen consistency, transfer the mixture from the freezer bowl into an air-tight container and keep in the freezer for at least 2 more hours.

PEANUT BUTTER AND BACON ICE CREAM

Yes, you read that right and it's exactly what it sounds like: creamy peanut butter swirled through creamy vanilla ice cream, with crumbled crispy fried real bacon in every bite. Sound strange? Maybe it is, but I guarantee that it's 100% delicious. This recipe was first suggested to me by a friend, who likes to frost vanilla cakes with peanut butter and bacon bits, and after giving it a try, I was instantly hooked. Bizarre as it may sound, this ice cream is definitely worth a try.

INGREDIENTS:

12 ounces of thin-cut pork bacon

1 cup of smooth peanut butter, softened

1 ½ cups of whole milk

1 ¼ cups of granulated sugar

2 cups of heavy cream

1 tablespoon of pure vanilla extract

INSTRUCTIONS:

1. Make sure your freezer is set at or below 0 degrees Fahrenheit (-18 degrees Celsius). Place the ice cream bowl attachment in the freezer for at least 15 hours.

2. Check that the ice cream bowl is completely frozen by giving it a shake before use. If you hear no movement, the bowl's cooling liquid is properly frozen.

3. In a large frying pan or skillet, fry the bacon on medium to high heat until crispy and brown.

4. Remove the bacon from the heat and blot the bacon thoroughly with paper towels to remove excess grease.
5. Crumble the bacon onto a paper towel and cover with another paper towel, to continue to absorb grease and preserve crispiness, and place in the refrigerator to chill for at least 1 hour.
6. Using your stand mixer and a mixing bowl, combine the milk and sugar until the sugar is fully dissolved in the milk.
7. Stir in the vanilla extract and the heavy cream. Stir thoroughly until all ingredients are evenly blended.
8. Fold in the softened peanut butter with several strokes to distribute it throughout the mixture in swirls, though do not attempt to fully blend in the peanut butter. Place the mixture in the refrigerator for 1-2 hours.
9. Take the ice cream freezer bowl out of the freezer and set it on the middle of your stand mixer's base.
10. Slide the assembly drive onto the bottom of the mixer head. Fit the dasher into the bowl and connect to the assembly drive.
11. When your stand mixer is prepared, switch it into "Level 1" or "Stir" mode. The dasher will begin to turn in the bowl. Pour the refrigerated mixture immediately from the mixing bowl into the freezer bowl.
12. After approximately 20 minutes (in the last five minutes of freezing), pour the crumbled crispy bacon directly into the freezer bowl to let mix completely.
13. After approximately 25-30 minutes (total), the mixture will have frozen to a thick, creamy soft-serve consistency, with the peanut butter and bacon laced throughout for salty-sweet deliciousness in every bite. Serve directly from the ice cream freezer bowl into bowls or cones, and enjoy!
14. For a more hard-frozen consistency, transfer the mixture from the freezer bowl into an air-tight container and keep in the freezer for at least 2 more hours.

MINT CHOCOLATE CHIP

This is such a classic ice cream shop favorite that I couldn't leave it out. Creamy, minty ice cream is laced with small chocolate pieces that seem to melt in your mouth. The best thing about making ice cream at home is making it to your specific taste so feel free to experiment with more mint flavoring or more chocolate pieces if that is what your tastebuds desire.

INGREDIENTS:

¾ cup of sugar

1 cup of whole milk

2 cups of heavy cream

1 ½ teaspoons pure peppermint extract

4 ounces semi-sweet chocolate bar, chopped

INSTRUCTIONS:

1. Make sure your freezer is set at or below 0 degrees Fahrenheit (-18 degrees Celsius). Place the ice cream bowl attachment in the freezer for at least 15 hours.

2. Check that the ice cream bowl is completely frozen by giving it a shake before use. If you hear no movement, the bowl's cooling liquid is properly frozen.

3. Using your stand mixer and a mixing bowl, blend the milk and sugar until the sugar is fully dissolved.

4. Add in the heavy cream and peppermint extract, and stir until all ingredients are evenly combined. Place the mixture in the refrigerator for 1-2 hours.

5. Take the ice cream freezer bowl out of the freezer and set it on the middle of your stand mixer's base.

6. Slide the assembly drive onto the bottom of the mixer head. Fit the dasher into the bowl and connect to the assembly drive.

7. When your stand mixer is prepared, switch it into "Level 1" or "Stir" mode. The dasher will begin to turn in the bowl. Pour the refrigerated mixture immediately from the mixing bowl into the freezer bowl.

8. After approximately 20 minutes (in the last five minutes of freezing), add the chopped chocolate pieces into the freezer bowl to let mix completely.

9. After approximately 25-30 minutes (total), the mixture will have frozen to a thick, creamy soft-serve consistency, laden with perfect melt in your mouth frozen mint chocolate candies. Serve directly from the ice cream freezer bowl into bowls or cones, and enjoy!

10. For a more hard-frozen consistency, transfer the mixture from the freezer bowl into an air-tight container and keep in the freezer for at least 2 more hours.

CAKE BATTER ICE CREAM

For the kid in you who just can't help licking the batter from the spoon every time you make a cake. Here is an easy, egg free frozen version that you can whip up quickly using your ice cream attachment. I've found the best taste comes from the Duncan Hines mix, but experiment to see if you have a favorite.

INGREDIENTS:

3 cups of heavy cream

1 cup of milk

¾ cup of sugar

¼ teaspoon of salt

½ cup of Duncan Hines Butter Cake Batter

INSTRUCTIONS:

1. Make sure your freezer is set at or below 0 degrees Fahrenheit (-18 degrees Celsius). Place the ice cream bowl attachment in the freezer for at least 15 hours.

2. Check that the ice cream bowl is completely frozen by giving it a shake before use. If you hear no movement, the bowl's cooling liquid is properly frozen.

3. In a large saucepan, mix 1 cup of heavy cream, salt and the sugar over a medium heat, stirring until the sugar is dissolved.

4. Remove from heat and stir in the dry cake mix. Mix well. Add the remaining heavy cream and milk.

5. Place in the refrigerator for at least 4 hours to let cake flavor develop. Re-stir the mixture before pouring into the ice cream freezer bowl.

6. Take the ice cream freezer bowl out of the freezer and set it on the middle of your stand mixer's base. Slide the assembly drive onto the bottom of the mixer head. Fit the dasher into the bowl and connect to the assembly drive.

7. When your stand mixer is prepared, switch it into "Level 1" or "Stir" mode. The dasher will begin to turn in the bowl. Pour the refrigerated mixture immediately from the mixing bowl into the freezer bowl.

8. After approximately 30 minutes, the mixture will have frozen to a creamy soft-serve consistency. Serve directly from the ice cream freezer bowl into serving bowls or cones, and enjoy!

9. For a more hard-frozen consistency, transfer the mixture from the freezer bowl into an air-tight container and keep in the freezer for at least 2 more hours.

DULCE DE LECHE ICE CREAM

This delicious concoction may sound swanky, but the taste is pure comforting sweetness. Dulce de leche is a creamy caramel sauce that is very easy to make at home using a can of sweetened condensed milk. Make your own dulce de leche and whip up a batch of this delicious ice cream today!

INGREDIENTS:

2 cups whole milk
1 cup heavy cream
1 ½ cups dulce de leche
½ cup of sugar
6 egg yolks
½ teaspoon vanilla extract
pinch of salt

INSTRUCTIONS:

1. Make sure your freezer is set at or below 0 degrees Fahrenheit (-18 degrees Celsius). Place the ice cream bowl attachment in the freezer for at least 15 hours.

2. Check that the ice cream bowl is completely frozen by giving it a shake before use. If you hear no movement, the bowl's cooling liquid is properly frozen.

3. In a large saucepan, mix the whole milk, heavy cream and 1 cup of dulce de leche over a medium heat, until steam is just beginning to rise.

4. Using your stand mixer and a mixing bowl, beat or whisk the sugar, egg yolks, salt and vanilla extract.

5. Reduce the speed of the mixer to a low speed, and add in one cup of the hot milk and cream mixture to the mixing bowl. Mix until evenly and smoothly blended.

6. Pour egg mixture into the saucepan with the warm cream and milk and thoroughly stir together.

7. Raise the heat under the saucepan to medium. Stir the mixture continuously with a wooden spoon, until the mixture has reached a custard-like consistency. Strain the custard from the saucepan into a medium sized bowl with a fine mesh strainer.

8. Bring the custard to room temperature and then cover and refrigerate for at least 1 hour.

9. Take the ice cream freezer bowl out of the freezer and set it on the middle of your stand mixer's base. Slide the assembly drive onto the bottom of the mixer head. Fit the dasher into the bowl and connect to the assembly drive.

10. When your stand mixer is prepared, switch it into "Level 1" or "Stir" mode. The dasher will begin to turn in the bowl. Pour the refrigerated mixture immediately from the mixing bowl into the freezer bowl.

11. After approximately 20 minutes (in the last five minutes of freezing), add the rest of the dulce de leche into the ice cream bowl to let mix completely.

12. After approximately 30 minutes, the mixture will have frozen to a dense, creamy soft-serve consistency. Serve directly from the ice cream freezer bowl into serving bowls or cones, and enjoy!

13. For a more hard-frozen consistency, transfer the mixture from the freezer bowl into an air-tight container and keep in the freezer for at least 2 more hours.

Blackberry Chunk Ice Cream

In my house, summer means two things: homemade ice cream, and fresh blackberries. So what better way to celebrate and preserve the tastes of the season than with this awesome ice cream recipe, laden with fresh blackberry juice and fruit? Just picked from the bush, from your local market and even frozen berries taste delicious in the recipe.

INGREDIENTS:

3 cups of fresh ripe blackberries, rinsed and patted dry, with large ones sliced in half

2 tablespoons of fresh lime juice

1 ½ cups of white sugar

1 ½ cups of whole milk

3 cups of heavy cream

2 teaspoons of pure vanilla extract

INSTRUCTIONS:

1. Make sure your freezer is set at or below 0 degrees Fahrenheit (-18 degrees Celsius). Place the ice cream bowl attachment in the freezer for at least 15 hours.

2. Check that the ice cream bowl is completely frozen by giving it a shake before use. If you hear no movement, the bowl's cooling liquid is properly frozen.

3. In a mixing bowl, stir the sliced blackberries, the lime juice, and ½ cup of the sugar. Stir until blackberries are fully coated and the lime juice and sugar are evenly blended, then leave to sit so that the

blackberries can soak up the lime and sugar for approximately two hours.

4. Strain the berries in a fine mesh sieve and conserve the juice.
5. Using a hand-masher, food processor or blender, mash or puree half of the berries until quite smooth.
6. Using your stand mixer and a mixing bowl, stir the milk with the remaining sugar, until the sugar is fully dissolved.
7. Stir in the vanilla extract, the heavy cream, the reserved berry juice and the mashed berries, stirring thoroughly until all ingredients are evenly combined. Chill in the refrigerator for 1-2 hours.
8. Take the ice cream freezer bowl out of the freezer and set it on the middle of your stand mixer's base.
9. Slide the assembly drive onto the bottom of the mixer head. Fit the dasher into the bowl and connect to the assembly drive.
10. When your stand mixer is prepared, switch it into "Level 1" or "Stir" mode. The dasher will begin to turn in the bowl. Pour the refrigerated mixture immediately from the mixing bowl into the freezer bowl.
11. After approximately 20 minutes (in the last five minutes of freezing), add the reserved sliced and strained blackberries into the ice cream bowl to let mix completely.
12. After approximately 25-30 minutes (total), the mixture will have frozen to a thick, creamy soft-serve consistency, with the frozen berry slices adding plenty of sweetness to every bite. Serve directly from the ice cream freezer bowl into serving bowls or cones, and enjoy!
13. For a more hard-frozen consistency, transfer the mixture from the freezer bowl into an air-tight container and keep in the freezer for at least 2 more hours.

S'MORES ICE CREAM

That old campfire favorite of graham crackers, toasted marshmallow, and melted chocolate gets a frozen update with this awesome ice cream, packed with chocolate and marshmallow swirls and crumbled graham cracker in every bite. No doubt about it, everyone will want s'more of this frozen goodie!

INGREDIENTS:

1 ½ cups of whole milk

1 ½ cups of white sugar

1 cup of softened marshmallow spread (any store bought brand or home preparation will do)

1 cup of chocolate syrup

2 ½ cups of heavy cream

1 teaspoon of pure vanilla extract

1 cup of crumbled graham crackers

INSTRUCTIONS:

1. Make sure your freezer is set at or below 0 degrees Fahrenheit (-18 degrees Celsius). Place the ice cream bowl attachment in the freezer for at least 15 hours.

2. Check that the ice cream bowl is completely frozen by giving it a shake before use. If you hear no movement, the bowl's cooling liquid is properly frozen.

3. Using your stand mixer and a mixing bowl, combine the milk and sugar until the sugar is fully dissolved.

4. Stir in the heavy cream and vanilla. Stir thoroughly until all ingredients are evenly blended. Place the mixture in the refrigerator for 2 hours.

5. Take the ice cream freezer bowl out of the freezer and set it on the middle of your stand mixer's base.

6. Slide the assembly drive onto the bottom of the mixer head. Fit the dasher into the bowl and connect to the assembly drive.

7. When your stand mixer is prepared, switch it into "Level 1" or "Stir" mode. The dasher will begin to turn in the bowl. Pour the refrigerated mixture immediately from the mixing bowl into the freezer bowl.

8. After approximately 20 minutes (in the last five minutes of freezing), pour in the softened marshmallow spread, the chocolate syrup, and the crumbled graham crackers into the freezer bowl to let mix completely.

9. After approximately 25-30 minutes (total), the mixture will have frozen to a thick, creamy soft-serve consistency, with the crumbled grahams, marshmallow, and chocolate swirled and embedded throughout for s'mores perfection. Serve directly from the ice cream freezer bowl into bowls or cones, and enjoy!

10. For a more hard-frozen consistency, transfer the mixture from the freezer bowl into an air-tight container and keep in the freezer for at least 2 more hours.

Smooth Mandarin Ice Cream

Mandarin oranges are just the most delightful fruit. They are the smaller, sweeter cousin to regular oranges, pure citrus goodness and best of all, they marry perfectly with fresh vanilla ice cream for a frozen confection that's both refreshing and delicious. Garnish with a little mandarin zest if you have some on hand, or a sprig of mint.

INGREDIENTS:

5 cups of mandarin oranges, peeled and sectioned

½ cup of white sugar

1 ½ cups of whole milk

2 ¾ cups of heavy cream

1 ½ teaspoons of pure vanilla extract

INSTRUCTIONS:

1. Make sure your freezer is set at or below 0 degrees Fahrenheit (-18 degrees Celsius). Place the ice cream bowl attachment in the freezer for at least 15 hours.

2. Check that the ice cream bowl is completely frozen by giving it a shake before use. If you hear no movement, the bowl's cooling liquid is properly frozen.

3. Using a hand-masher, food processor or blender, mash or puree half of the mandarins until quite smooth, discarding the pulp and fibers.

4. Using your stand mixer and a mixing bowl, stir the milk with the sugar, until the sugar is fully dissolved.

5. Stir in the vanilla extract, the heavy cream and the mashed mandarins and any juice, stirring thoroughly until all ingredients are evenly combined. Chill in the refrigerator for 1-2 hours.
6. Take the ice cream freezer bowl out of the freezer and set it on the middle of your stand mixer's base.
7. Slide the assembly drive onto the bottom of the mixer head. Fit the dasher into the bowl and connect to the assembly drive.
8. When your stand mixer is prepared, switch it into "Level 1" or "Stir" mode. The dasher will begin to turn in the bowl. Pour the refrigerated mixture immediately from the mixing bowl into the freezer bowl.
9. After approximately 20 minutes (in the last five minutes of freezing), pour in the remaining mandarin chunks through the ingredient spout on the appliance's lid
10. After approximately 25-30 minutes (total), the mixture will have frozen to a thick, creamy soft-serve consistency, laced with sweet citrus mandarin goodness in every bite. Serve directly from the ice cream freezer bowl into serving bowls or cones, and enjoy!
11. For a more hard-frozen consistency, transfer the mixture from the freezer bowl into an air-tight container and keep in the freezer for at least 2 more hours.

ROCKY ROAD ICE CREAM

This classic combination of chocolate ice cream, chopped walnuts, and mini marshmallows is a frozen favorite for good reason. The original chunky ice cream is readily available in stores, but I promise it's more fun and more delicious when it comes out of your own kitchen. So have at it and get yourself some rocky road!

INGREDIENTS:

1 cup of unsweetened dark cocoa powder

1 cup of white sugar

1 ¼ cups of whole milk

3 cups of heavy cream

1 tablespoon of pure vanilla extract

1 cup of chopped walnuts

1 cup of mini marshmallows

INSTRUCTIONS:

1. Make sure your freezer is set at or below 0 degrees Fahrenheit (-18 degrees Celsius). Place the ice cream bowl attachment in the freezer for at least 15 hours.

2. Check that the ice cream bowl is completely frozen by giving it a shake before use. If you hear no movement, the bowl's cooling liquid is properly frozen.

3. Using your stand mixer and a mixing bowl, combine the cocoa and sugar, and stir until evenly combined. Add the whole milk, and combine until the cocoa and sugar are fully dissolved in the milk.

4. Stir in the vanilla extract and the heavy cream. Stir thoroughly until all ingredients are evenly blended. Place the mixture in the refrigerator for 1-2 hours.
5. Take the ice cream freezer bowl out of the freezer and set it on the middle of your stand mixer's base.
6. Slide the assembly drive onto the bottom of the mixer head. Fit the dasher into the bowl and connect to the assembly drive.
7. When your stand mixer is prepared, switch it into "Level 1" or "Stir" mode. The dasher will begin to turn in the bowl. Pour the refrigerated mixture immediately from the mixing bowl into the freezer bowl.
8. After approximately 20 minutes (in the last five minutes of freezing), pour in the chopped walnuts and mini marshmallows into the freezer bowl to let mix completely.
9. After approximately 25-30 minutes (total), the mixture will have frozen to a thick, creamy soft-serve consistency, with every chocolaty scoop packed with marshmallows and walnuts! Serve directly from the ice cream freezer bowl into bowls or cones, and enjoy!
10. For a more hard-frozen consistency, transfer the mixture from the freezer bowl into an air-tight container and keep in the freezer for at least 2 more hours.

DREAMY CHOCOLATE ICE CREAM

Sometimes you just crave simple chocolate ice cream. This ice cream is chocolatey without being too rich and is so simple to whip up and satisfy your chocolate cravings. Enjoy it just as it is or add your favorite toppings.

INGREDIENTS:

1 cup Dutch process chocolate cocoa

½ cup brown sugar

⅔ cup white sugar

1 ½ cups whole milk

3 ¼ cup heavy cream

2 tablespoons of pure vanilla extract

INSTRUCTIONS:

1. Make sure your freezer is set at or below 0 degrees Fahrenheit (-18 degrees Celsius). Place the ice cream bowl attachment in the freezer for at least 15 hours.

2. Check that the ice cream bowl is completely frozen by giving it a shake before use. If you hear no movement, the bowl's cooling liquid is properly frozen.

3. Using your stand mixer and a mixing bowl, combine the chocolate cocoa with the brown and white sugar. Stir in the milk until the sugar is fully dissolved in the milk.

4. Stir in the vanilla extract and the heavy cream. Stir thoroughly until all ingredients are evenly blended.

5. Take the ice cream freezer bowl out of the freezer and set it on the middle of your stand mixer's base.

6. Slide the assembly drive onto the bottom of the mixer head. Fit the dasher into the bowl and connect to the assembly drive.

7. When your stand mixer is prepared, switch it into "Level 1" or "Stir" mode. The dasher will begin to turn in the bowl. Pour the chocolate mixture immediately from the mixing bowl into the freezer bowl.

8. After approximately 25-30 minutes (total), the mixture will have frozen to a thick, creamy soft-serve consistency, the perfect chocolate ice cream to eat by itself or decorated with your favorite topping. Serve directly from the ice cream freezer bowl into bowls or cones, and enjoy!

9. For a more hard-frozen consistency, transfer the mixture from the freezer bowl into an air-tight container and keep in the freezer for at least 2 more hours.

Raspberry Fudge Swirl Ice Cream

This fruity, chocolaty ice cream is an absolute delight. It is simple to prepare, and a whole lot of fun to eat. The flavor combination of raspberry sauce with dense chocolate fudge embedded in vanilla ice cream will be enjoyed by kids and adults alike.

INGREDIENTS:

1 cup of dense chocolate fudge, chilled and sliced into bite-sized chunks

1 cup of smooth raspberry sauce or syrup (any homemade or store bought preparation will do)

1 ½ cups of whole milk

1 ¼ cups of granulated sugar

2 cups of heavy cream

1 tablespoon of pure vanilla extract

INSTRUCTIONS:

1. Make sure your freezer is set at or below 0 degrees Fahrenheit (-18 degrees Celsius). Place the ice cream bowl attachment in the freezer for at least 15 hours.
2. Check that the ice cream bowl is completely frozen by giving it a shake before use. If you hear no movement, the bowl's cooling liquid is properly frozen.
3. Using your stand mixer and a mixing bowl, combine the milk and sugar at a low speed until the sugar is fully dissolved in the milk.
4. Stir in the vanilla extract and the heavy cream. Stir thoroughly until all ingredients are evenly blended.

5. Fold in the raspberry sauce with several strokes to distribute it throughout the mixture in swirls, though do not attempt to fully blend in the raspberry sauce. Allow mixture to chill in the refrigerator for 1-2 hours.

6. Take the ice cream freezer bowl out of the freezer and set it on the middle of your stand mixer's base.

7. Slide the assembly drive onto the bottom of the mixer head. Fit the dasher into the bowl and connect to the assembly drive.

8. When your stand mixer is prepared, switch it into "Level 1" or "Stir" mode. The dasher will begin to turn in the bowl. Pour the refrigerated mixture immediately from the mixing bowl into the freezer bowl.

9. After approximately 20 minutes (in the last five minutes of freezing), pour the chunks of fudge directly into the freezer bowl to let mix completely.

10. After approximately 25-30 minutes (total), the mixture will have frozen to a thick, creamy soft-serve consistency, with the raspberry sauce and chocolate fudge swirling throughout in every bite. Serve directly from the ice cream freezer bowl into bowls or cones, and enjoy!

11. For a more hard-frozen consistency, transfer the mixture from the freezer bowl into an air-tight container and keep in the freezer for at least 2 more hours.

PINEAPPLE UPSIDE-DOWN CAKE ICE CREAM

Although its not exactly a cake, this ice cream brings together all the flavors of the traditional pineapple upside down cake in a frozen concoction. You'll find the goodness of pineapple, candied cherries, and delicious vanilla cake in every sweet frozen bite. My family absolutely loves this cold confection, and I know yours will too.

INGREDIENTS:

1 ½ cups of whole milk

1 cup of white sugar

2 tablespoons of light molasses

1 cup of pineapple (fresh and peeled, or canned and drained), chopped into small bite sized chunks

½ cup of maraschino cherries, drained

2 ½ cups of heavy cream

1 ½ teaspoons of pure vanilla extract

1 cup of white sponge cake (homemade and chilled, or store bought), cut into bite sized chunks

INSTRUCTIONS:

1. Make sure your freezer is set at or below 0 degrees Fahrenheit (-18 degrees Celsius). Place the ice cream bowl attachment in the freezer for at least 15 hours.

2. Check that the ice cream bowl is completely frozen by giving it a shake before use. If you hear no movement, the bowl's cooling liquid is properly frozen.

3. Using your stand mixer and a mixing bowl, combine the milk, sugar and molasses until the sugar is fully dissolved.

4. Stir in the heavy cream and vanilla. Stir thoroughly until all ingredients are evenly blended. Place in the refrigerator for 1-2 hours.

5. Take the ice cream freezer bowl out of the freezer and set it on the middle of your stand mixer's base.

6. Slide the assembly drive onto the bottom of the mixer head. Fit the dasher into the bowl and connect to the assembly drive.

7. When your stand mixer is prepared, switch it into "Level 1" or "Stir" mode. The dasher will begin to turn in the bowl. Pour the refrigerated mixture immediately from the mixing bowl into the freezer bowl.

8. After approximately 20 minutes (in the last five minutes of freezing), add the chunks of pineapple, cake, and the maraschino cherries into the freezer bowl to let mix completely.

9. After approximately 25-30 minutes (total), the mixture will have frozen to a thick, creamy soft-serve consistency, with the pineapple, cherries, and cake perfectly frozen and laced through every delicious scoop. Serve directly from the ice cream freezer bowl into bowls or cones, and enjoy!

10. For a more hard-frozen consistency, transfer the mixture from the freezer bowl into an air-tight container and keep in the freezer for at least 2 more hours.

CHILI CHOCOLATE ICE CREAM

This one may sound a little odd, but trust me, it's absolutely delicious. The combination of decadent dark chocolate with spicy red pepper and chili powder is absolutely irresistible. The decadent, cold, chocolate ice cream packs a surprising punch of heat with the addition of the chili and red pepper. For those dessert lovers who crave a little something spicy and kicky with their treats, this is a great choice

INGREDIENTS:

1 cup of unsweetened dark cocoa powder

1/2 cup of white sugar

1/4 cup of packed brown sugar

1 1/2 cups of whole milk

3 1/4 cups of heavy cream

1 tablespoon of dried chili powder

1/2 tablespoon of ground red pepper flakes

INSTRUCTIONS:

1. Make sure your freezer is set at or below 0 degrees Fahrenheit (-18 degrees Celsius). Place the ice cream bowl attachment in the freezer for at least 15 hours.

2. Check that the ice cream bowl is completely frozen by giving it a shake before use. If you hear no movement, the bowl's cooling liquid is properly frozen.

3. Using your stand mixer and a mixing bowl, combine the cocoa, brown and white sugar, and stir until evenly combined.

4. Add the whole milk, and combine until the cocoa and sugars are fully dissolved in the milk.

5. Stir in the chili powder, the red pepper flakes, and the heavy cream. Stir thoroughly until all ingredients are evenly blended.

6. Take the ice cream freezer bowl out of the freezer and set it on the middle of your stand mixer's base.

7. Slide the assembly drive onto the bottom of the mixer head. Fit the dasher into the bowl and connect to the assembly drive.

8. When your stand mixer is prepared, switch it into "Level 1" or "Stir" mode. The dasher will begin to turn in the bowl. Pour the refrigerated mixture immediately from the mixing bowl into the freezer bowl.

9. After approximately 25-30 minutes, the mixture will have frozen to a thick, creamy soft-serve consistency. Serve directly from the ice cream freezer bowl into serving bowls or cones, and enjoy!

10. For a more hard-frozen consistency, transfer the mixture from the freezer bowl into an air-tight container and keep in the freezer for at least 2 more hours.

GELATO

For the longest time – too long – I didn't know the difference between ice cream and gelato. Privately, I didn't even think there was any real difference, other than a foreign name that made one sound fancier than the other. Then I had the privilege of tasting real gelato, made by an Italian American friend in her own home freezing appliance, and only then did I realize how wrong I'd been about gelato.

Gelato is at once sweeter, denser, and more flavorful than most store bought ice creams. That's largely due to the cooking method in the preparations of the ingredients prior to freezing. The result is a frozen confection that contains less air – and more unadulterated taste – than with regular ice creams. For all of that, trust me, it's not that difficult, and all the recipes in this section contain full instructions for the pre-freezing cooking preparations that will ensure your gelato comes out just perfectly.

Needless to say, that high density flavor packed aspect of gelato makes it an ideal palate for creative experimentation. From traditional favorite flavor combos like salted toffee and peaches and cream, to more exotic tastes such as passion fruit and rosehips, the gelatos in this section are each a masterpiece unto themselves. These recipes are the perfect way to elevate a sophisticated dinner party, or just give your taste buds their own private party! Either way, real gelato – made with fresh ingredients, right in your own kitchen – is a gastronomic luxury not to be missed.

Creamy Hibiscus Gelato

If you've never tasted hibiscus tea, this gelato is seriously worth a try. The musky, sweet and sour hibiscus fragrance is utterly unique, unlike any other taste, and truly spectacular. That complex flavor is beautifully showcased in this luscious gelato – a genuine taste sensation in every bite.

INGREDIENTS:

3 ¼ cups of whole milk

8 hibiscus tea bags

1 cup of white sugar

1 cup of heavy cream

8 large egg yolks (separated from the whites)

¼ cup of fat free powdered milk

INSTRUCTIONS:

1. Make sure your freezer is set at or below 0 degrees Fahrenheit (-18 degrees Celsius). Place the ice cream bowl attachment in the freezer for at least 15 hours.

2. Check that the ice cream bowl is completely frozen by giving it a shake before use. If you hear no movement, the bowl's cooling liquid is properly frozen.

3. Pour the milk into a saucepan and heat until it's at a low simmer.

4. In a medium sized bowl, pour half of the warmed milk over the tea bags, and set to steep for 30 minutes.

5. After 30 minutes, strain the bowl with the tea bags, and squeeze out all the liquid from the tea bags.

6. Pour the powdered milk into the milk that remains in the saucepan, and stir gently over a low heat.
7. In your stand mixer or a mixing bowl, mix the egg yolks and the sugar, until evenly combined and thickened.
8. Pour the egg and sugar mixture back into the saucepan, and thoroughly stir together with the warming milk.
9. Add the tea infused milk into the saucepan, and raise the heat to medium. Stir the mixture continuously with a wooden spoon, until the mixture has reached a custard-like consistency.
10. Strain the custard from the saucepan into a medium sized bowl.
11. Stir in the cream until thoroughly combined, then cover and refrigerate for at least 6 hours.
12. Take the ice cream freezer bowl out of the freezer and set it on the middle of your stand mixer's base.
13. Slide the assembly drive onto the bottom of the mixer head. Fit the dasher into the bowl and connect to the assembly drive.
14. When your stand mixer is prepared, switch it into "Level 1" or "Stir" mode. The dasher will begin to turn in the bowl. Pour the refrigerated mixture immediately from the mixing bowl into the freezer bowl.
15. After approximately 25-30 minutes, the mixture will have frozen to a thick, creamy soft-serve consistency. Serve directly from the ice cream freezer bowl into serving bowls or cones, and enjoy!
16. For a more hard-frozen consistency, transfer the mixture from the freezer bowl into an air-tight container and keep in the freezer for at least 2 more hours.

Classic Vanilla-Custard Gelato

Gelato is, essentially, a frozen custard. The egg yolks are what make this dessert so rich and luxurious as compared to regular ice cream. This recipe presents the classic vanilla custard flavor of the traditional gelato in all its glory.

INGREDIENTS:

1 whole vanilla bean

1 cup of white sugar

2 ½ cups of half and half

8 large egg yolks (separated from the whites)

¼ cup of fat free powdered milk

1 cup of heavy cream

1 ½ teaspoon of pure vanilla extract

INSTRUCTIONS:

1. Make sure your freezer is set at or below 0 degrees Fahrenheit (-18 degrees Celsius). Place the ice cream bowl attachment in the freezer for at least 15 hours.

2. Check that the ice cream bowl is completely frozen by giving it a shake before use. If you hear no movement, the bowl's cooling liquid is properly frozen.

3. In a saucepan of at least 2 ½ quarts capacity, place the sugar and 1 ¼ cups of the half and half to simmer over a medium heat. Stir continuously and, once the sugar is fully dissolved, adjust the heat to low to keep the mixture warm.

4. Using a sharp knife, split the vanilla bean down the middle lengthwise, then use the blunt end of the knife to scrape out the seeds of the bean.
5. Stir the seeds and the bean pod into the heating sugar and half and half mixture in the saucepan, and simmer on a low heat for approximately 30 minutes.
6. Extract the vanilla bean pod and discard it, and keep the heat under the saucepan set to low.
7. Using your stand mixer and a mixing bowl,, whisk or whip the egg yolks for approximately 2 minutes until they're thickened.
8. While whisking the egg yolks, add in ½ cup of the hot mixture, and whisk thoroughly until all ingredients are completely combined.
9. Pour the egg yolks mixture into the saucepan with the rest of the vanilla infused half and half and sugar, and raise the heat under the saucepan back up to medium.
10. Continuously stir the mixture in the saucepan with a wooden spoon, until it has thickened to custard-like consistency.
11. Stir in the remaining half and half, vanilla extract, heavy cream and the powdered milk, and continue to stir for a few more minutes.
12. Remove the saucepan from the heat and strain the mixture through a fine mesh sieve into a large mixing bowl. Then cover the mixing bowl and refrigerate for at least 6 hours.
13. Take the ice cream freezer bowl out of the freezer and set it on the middle of your stand mixer's base.
14. Slide the assembly drive onto the bottom of the mixer head. Fit the dasher into the bowl and connect to the assembly drive.
15. When your stand mixer is prepared, switch it into "Level 1" or "Stir" mode. The dasher will begin to turn in the bowl. Pour the refrigerated mixture immediately from the mixing bowl into the freezer bowl.

16. After approximately 25-30 minutes, the mixture will have frozen to a thick, creamy soft-serve consistency. Serve directly from the ice cream freezer bowl into serving bowls or cones, and enjoy!

17. For a more hard-frozen consistency, transfer the mixture from the freezer bowl into an air-tight container and keep in the freezer for at least 2 more hours.

BANANA-CREAM GELATO

If you like banana cream pie, you'll absolutely love this banana cream gelato. The vanilla cream and the banana are a classic flavor blend, but what really makes this preparation special is the dense, rich, custard-like consistency of the gelato base – banana-cream heaven in every taste!

INGREDIENTS:

3 ¼ cups of whole milk

4 large ripe bananas, peeled, sliced and thoroughly mashed

1 cup of white sugar

1 cup of heavy cream

8 large egg yolks (separated from the whites)

¼ cup of fat free powdered milk

INSTRUCTIONS:

1. Make sure your freezer is set at or below 0 degrees Fahrenheit (-18 degrees Celsius). Place the ice cream bowl attachment in the freezer for at least 15 hours.

2. Check that the ice cream bowl is completely frozen by giving it a shake before use. If you hear no movement, the bowl's cooling liquid is properly frozen.

3. Pour the milk into a saucepan and heat until it's at a low simmer.

4. In a medium sized bowl, pour half of the warmed milk over the mashed banana, and whisk or beat thoroughly until evenly combined and fully blended.

5. Pour the powdered milk into the milk that remains in the saucepan, and stir gently over a low heat.

6. In a mixing bowl, whisk the egg yolks and the sugar, until evenly combined and thickened.

7. Pour the egg and sugar mixture into the saucepan, and thoroughly stir together with the warming milk.

8. Add the mashed banana and milk mixture into the saucepan, and raise the heat to medium. Stir the mixture continuously with a wooden spoon, until the mixture has reached a custard-like consistency and the banana becomes fragrant.

9. Strain the custard from the saucepan into a medium sized bowl.

10. Stir in the cream until thoroughly combined, then cover and refrigerate for at least 6 hours.

11. Take the ice cream freezer bowl out of the freezer and set it on the middle of your stand mixer's base.

12. Slide the assembly drive onto the bottom of the mixer head. Fit the dasher into the bowl and connect to the assembly drive.

13. When your stand mixer is prepared, switch it into "Level 1" or "Stir" mode. The dasher will begin to turn in the bowl. Pour the refrigerated mixture immediately from the mixing bowl into the freezer bowl.

14. After approximately 25-30 minutes, the mixture will have frozen to a thick, creamy soft-serve consistency. Serve directly from the ice cream freezer bowl into serving bowls or cones, and enjoy!

Strawberry Honeysuckle Gelato

The delicate flavor blend in this gelato is really amazing – perfect for a satisfying yet sophisticated cold treat on a hot day. If you can get your hands on honeysuckle flowers (try your local health food or organic food store) and ripe strawberries, this recipe is an absolute must try.

INGREDIENTS:

4 cups of ripe red strawberries (pre-thawed if frozen), rinsed and patted dry

1 cup of white sugar

2 tablespoons of dried edible honeysuckle flowers

2 ½ cups of half and half

6 large egg yolks (separated from the whites)

¼ cup of fat free powdered milk

1 cup of heavy cream

1 ½ teaspoons of pure vanilla extract

INSTRUCTIONS:

1. Make sure your freezer is set at or below 0 degrees Fahrenheit (-18 degrees Celsius). Place the ice cream bowl attachment in the freezer for at least 15 hours.

2. Check that the ice cream bowl is completely frozen by giving it a shake before use. If you hear no movement, the bowl's cooling liquid is properly frozen.

3. In a food processor or blender, puree the strawberries until thoroughly smooth.

4. Strain the strawberry puree through a fine mesh sieve, then discard the seeds and keep the approximately 2 cups that will have strained through.

5. In a saucepan at least 2 ½ quarts in capacity, place the sugar and 1 ¼ cups of the half and half to simmer over a medium heat. Stir continuously and, once the sugar is fully dissolved, adjust the heat to low to keep the mixture warm.

6. Using your stand mixer and a mixing bowl, whisk or whip the egg yolks for approximately 2 minutes until they're thickened.

7. While whisking the egg yolks, add in ½ cup of the hot half and half and sugar mixture, and whisk thoroughly until all ingredients are completely combined.

8. Pour the mixture with the egg yolks, into the saucepan with the rest of the half and half and sugar, and raise the heat under the saucepan back up to medium.

9. Continuously stir the mixture in the saucepan with a wooden spoon, until it has thickened to custard-like consistency.

10. Stir in the remaining half and half, the powdered milk, the heavy cream, and the dried edible honeysuckle.

11. Continue to stir for a few more minutes until the honeysuckle becomes fragrant, then remove the saucepan from the heat and strain the mixture through a fine mesh strainer into a large mixing bowl, discarding the flower husks.

12. Stir in the reserved strawberry puree and vanilla extract, then cover the mixing bowl and refrigerate for at least 6 hours.

13. Take the ice cream freezer bowl out of the freezer and set it on the middle of your stand mixer's base.

14. Slide the assembly drive onto the bottom of the mixer head. Fit the dasher into the bowl and connect to the assembly drive.

15. When your stand mixer is prepared, switch it into "Level 1" or "Stir" mode. The dasher will begin to turn in the bowl. Pour the

refrigerated mixture immediately from the mixing bowl into the freezer bowl.

16. After approximately 25-30 minutes, the mixture will have frozen to a thick, creamy soft-serve consistency. Serve directly from the ice cream freezer bowl into serving bowls or cones, and enjoy!

17. For a more hard-frozen consistency, transfer the mixture from the freezer bowl into an air-tight container and keep in the freezer for at least 2 more hours.

LILY CHARLES

SALTED TOFFEE GELATO

This wonderful gelato recipe has all the indulgent buttery goodness of sticky salted toffee but frozen into a consistency that won't leave you picking it out of your teeth! This gelato is a wonderful special occasion dessert to have in your freezer, for birthdays, parties, or any gathering where you really want to give people's sweet teeth a treat.

INGREDIENTS:

1 cup of old fashioned butter toffee, softened

1 cup of white sugar

2 ½ cups of half and half

6 large egg yolks (separated from the whites)

½ cup of salted butter, softened

2 teaspoons of salt

¼ cup of fat free powdered milk

1 cup of heavy cream

1 teaspoon of pure vanilla extract

INSTRUCTIONS:

1. Make sure your freezer is set at or below 0 degrees Fahrenheit (-18 degrees Celsius). Place the ice cream bowl attachment in the freezer for at least 15 hours.

2. Check that the ice cream bowl is completely frozen by giving it a shake before use. If you hear no movement, the bowl's cooling liquid is properly frozen.

3. In a saucepan at least 2 ½ quarts in capacity, place the sugar and 1 ¼ cups of the half and half to simmer over a medium heat. Stir continuously and, once the sugar is fully dissolved, adjust the heat to low to keep the mixture warm.

4. Stir the softened toffee and the softened butter into the saucepan with the sugar and the half and half, and simmer on a low heat for approximately 30 minutes.

5. Using your stand mixer and a mixing bowl, whisk or whip the egg yolks for approximately 2 minutes until they're thickened.

6. While whisking the egg yolks, add in ½ cup of the hot mixture, and whisk thoroughly until all ingredients are completely combined.

7. Pour the mixture with the egg yolks back into the saucepan with the rest of the warm mixture, and raise the heat under the saucepan back up to medium.

8. Continuously stir the mixture in the saucepan with a wooden spoon, until it has thickened to custard-like consistency.

9. Stir in the remaining half and half, the salt, heavy cream and the powdered milk. Continue to stir for a few more minutes.

10. Remove the saucepan from the heat and strain the mixture through a fine mesh sieve into a large mixing bowl.

11. Cover the mixing bowl and refrigerate for at least 6 hours.

12. Take the ice cream freezer bowl out of the freezer and set it on the middle of your stand mixer's base.

13. Slide the assembly drive onto the bottom of the mixer head. Fit the dasher into the bowl and connect to the assembly drive.

14. When your stand mixer is prepared, switch it into "Level 1" or "Stir" mode. The dasher will begin to turn in the bowl. Pour the refrigerated mixture immediately from the mixing bowl into the freezer bowl.

15. After approximately 25-30 minutes, the mixture will have frozen to a thick, creamy soft-serve consistency. Serve directly from the ice cream freezer bowl into serving bowls or cones, and enjoy!

16. For a more hard-frozen consistency, transfer the mixture from the freezer bowl into an air-tight container and keep in the freezer for at least 2 more hours.

COCONUT CREAM GELATO

If you like coconut cream pie, you'll absolutely love this frozen rendition, in which the coconut and cream are perfectly distilled in this rich, dense gelato. This is a great dessert any time of year, and I especially love it around the holidays, when decorative coconut shaving garnishes look like white Christmas snow! Enjoy.

INGREDIENTS:

1 cup of shaved coconut (any store bought brand will do, as long as it's unsweetened)

1 cup of white sugar

1 ½ cups of half and half

1 cup of coconut milk

8 large egg yolks (separated from the whites)

¼ cup of fat free powdered milk

1 cup of heavy cream

½ teaspoon of pure vanilla extract

INSTRUCTIONS:

1. Make sure your freezer is set at or below 0 degrees Fahrenheit (-18 degrees Celsius). Place the ice cream bowl attachment in the freezer for at least 15 hours.
2. Check that the ice cream bowl is completely frozen by giving it a shake before use. If you hear no movement, the bowl's cooling liquid is properly frozen.
3. In a saucepan at least 2 ½ quarts large, bring the sugar and 1 cup of the half and half to simmer over a medium heat. Stir continuously and, once the sugar is fully dissolved, adjust the heat to low to keep the mixture warm.
4. Stir the shaved coconut into the heating sugar and half and half mixture in the saucepan, and simmer on a low heat for approximately 30 minutes.
5. Using your stand mixer and a mixing bowl, whisk or whip the egg yolks for approximately 2 minutes until they're thickened.
6. While whisking the egg yolks, add in ½ cup of the hot mixture, and whisk thoroughly until all ingredients are completely combined.
7. Pour the mixture with the egg yolks into the saucepan with the rest of the coconut infused half and half and sugar, and raise the heat under the saucepan back up to medium.
8. Add the coconut milk to the saucepan, and continuously stir the mixture with a wooden spoon, until it has thickened to custard-like consistency and the coconut has become fragrant.
9. Stir in the remaining half and half, heavy cream and the powdered milk, and continue to stir for a few more minutes.
10. Remove the saucepan from the heat and strain the mixture through a fine mesh sieve into a large mixing bowl, discarding the husks of the coconut shavings. Blend in vanilla extract.
11. Cover the mixing bowl and refrigerate for at least 6 hours.

12. Take the ice cream freezer bowl out of the freezer and set it on the middle of your stand mixer's base.

13. Slide the assembly drive onto the bottom of the mixer head. Fit the dasher into the bowl and connect to the assembly drive.

14. When your stand mixer is prepared, switch it into "Level 1" or "Stir" mode. The dasher will begin to turn in the bowl. Pour the refrigerated mixture immediately from the mixing bowl into the freezer bowl.

15. After approximately 25-30 minutes, the mixture will have frozen to a thick, creamy soft-serve consistency. Serve directly from the ice cream freezer bowl into serving bowls or cones, and enjoy!

16. For a more hard-frozen consistency, transfer the mixture from the freezer bowl into an air-tight container and keep in the freezer for at least 2 more hours.

LILY CHARLES

PEACHES AND CREAM GELATO

Peaches and cream are an old favorite of mine from childhood – such simple, sweet flavors, which pair together so perfectly. This is the perfect ice cream to prepare in the summer when peaches are ripe and plentiful.

INGREDIENTS:

1 ½ pounds of fresh peaches, peeled and cubed (thawed, if frozen)

½ cup of peach nectar

2 cups of whole milk

1 cup of white sugar

¼ cup of fat free powdered milk

2 cups of light cream

8 large egg yolks (separated from the whites)

1 teaspoon of pure vanilla extract

INSTRUCTIONS:

1. Make sure your freezer is set at or below 0 degrees Fahrenheit (-18 degrees Celsius). Place the ice cream bowl attachment in the freezer for at least 15 hours.

2. Check that the ice cream bowl is completely frozen by giving it a shake before use. If you hear no movement, the bowl's cooling liquid is properly frozen.

3. In a food processor or blender, puree the peaches until thoroughly smooth.

4. Strain the peach puree through a fine mesh sieve, discarding the pulp, and keep the approximately 2 ½ cups of peach puree that will have strained through.
5. Stir the peach nectar in with the strained puree, combine thoroughly, then cover and refrigerate for at least 30 minutes.
6. In a large saucepan, combine the milk, sugar, and powdered milk, bringing to simmer over a medium heat. Stir continuously and, once the sugar is fully dissolved, adjust the heat to low to keep the mixture warm.
7. Using your stand mixer and a mixing bowl, whisk or whip the egg yolks for approximately 2 minutes until they're thickened.
8. While whisking the egg yolks, slowly stir in 1 cup of the sugar and hot milk mixture from the saucepan, and whisk thoroughly until all ingredients are completely combined.
9. Pour the mixture with the egg yolks back into the saucepan with the rest of the milk and sugar, and raise the heat under the saucepan back up to medium.
10. Continuously stir the mixture in the saucepan with a wooden spoon, until it has thickened to a custard-like consistency.
11. Continue to stir for a few more minutes, then remove the saucepan from the heat and strain the custard-like mixture through a fine mesh strainer into a large mixing bowl.
12. Stir in the reserved peach puree, the light cream, and the vanilla extract and mix until all ingredients are fully combined.
13. Cover the mixing bowl and refrigerate for at least 6 hours.
14. Take the ice cream freezer bowl out of the freezer and set it on the middle of your stand mixer's base.
15. Slide the assembly drive onto the bottom of the mixer head. Fit the dasher into the bowl and connect to the assembly drive.
16. When your stand mixer is prepared, switch it into "Level 1" or "Stir" mode. The dasher will begin to turn in the bowl. Pour the

refrigerated mixture immediately from the mixing bowl into the freezer bowl.

17. After approximately 25-30 minutes, the mixture will have frozen to a thick, creamy soft-serve consistency. Serve directly from the ice cream freezer bowl into serving bowls or cones, and enjoy!

18. For a more hard-frozen consistency, transfer the mixture from the freezer bowl into an air-tight container and keep in the freezer for at least 2 more hours.

Chocolate Cheesecake Gelato

I happen to have a serious weakness for chocolate cheesecake, but I am truly powerless over my craving for the following recipe, which freezes that irresistible chocolate cheesecake flavor into a perfectly dense, rich gelato. Proceed with caution – one scoop of this chocolate cheesecake bliss is never enough.

INGREDIENTS:

1 whole vanilla bean

1 cup of white sugar

1 ½ cups of half and half

1 cup of regular cream cheese, softened

2 large egg yolks (separated from the whites)

¼ cup of fat free powdered milk

1 cup of heavy cream

1 cup of Dutch process cocoa powder

½ teaspoon of pure vanilla extract

INSTRUCTIONS:

1. Make sure your freezer is set at or below 0 degrees Fahrenheit (-18 degrees Celsius). Place the ice cream bowl attachment in the freezer for at least 15 hours.
2. Check that the ice cream bowl is completely frozen by giving it a shake before use. If you hear no movement, the bowl's cooling liquid is properly frozen.
3. In a saucepan at least 2 ½ quarts in capacity, place the sugar and ¾ cups of the half and half to simmer over a medium heat. Stir continuously and, once the sugar is fully dissolved, adjust the heat to low to keep the mixture warm.
4. Using a sharp knife, split the vanilla bean down the middle lengthwise, then use the blunt end of the knife to scrape out the seeds of the bean.
5. Stir the seeds and the bean pod into the heating sugar and half and half mixture in the saucepan, and simmer on a low heat for approximately 30 minutes.
6. Extract the vanilla bean pod and discard it, and keep the heat under the saucepan set to low.
7. Using your stand mixer and a mixing bowl, whisk or whip the egg yolks for approximately 2 minutes until they're thickened.
8. While whisking the egg yolks, add in ½ cup of the hot mixture, and whisk thoroughly until all ingredients are completely combined.
9. Pour the mixture with the egg yolks into the saucepan with the rest of the vanilla-infused half and half and sugar, and raise the heat under the saucepan back up to medium.
10. Continuously stir the mixture in the saucepan with a wooden spoon, until it has thickened to a custard-like consistency.

11. Stir in the remaining half and half and the powdered milk, and continue to stir for a few more minutes.

12. Remove the saucepan from the heat and strain the mixture through a fine mesh sieve into a large mixing bowl.

13. Combine the softened cream cheese, heavy cream, vanilla extract and the cocoa powder with the mixture. Use your stand mixer and stir until all ingredients are evenly combined (about 2 minutes).

14. Cover the mixing bowl and refrigerate for at least 6 hours.

15. Take the ice cream freezer bowl out of the freezer and set it on the middle of your stand mixer's base.

16. Slide the assembly drive onto the bottom of the mixer head. Fit the dasher into the bowl and connect to the assembly drive.

17. When your stand mixer is prepared, switch it into "Level 1" or "Stir" mode. The dasher will begin to turn in the bowl. Pour the refrigerated mixture immediately from the mixing bowl into the freezer bowl.

18. After approximately 25-30 minutes, the mixture will have frozen to a thick, creamy soft-serve consistency. Serve directly from the ice cream freezer bowl into serving bowls or cones, and enjoy!

19. For a more hard-frozen consistency, transfer the mixture from the freezer bowl into an air-tight container and keep in the freezer for at least 2 more hours.

LILY CHARLES

RASPBERRY LAVENDER GELATO

The amazing flavor blend in this gelato is sophisticated, sumptuous, and simply irresistible. The tart tang of the raspberries is complimented perfectly by the fragrant lavender. Frozen and blended into a perfect soft-serve dessert, this is the perfect item to have in your freezer for those occasions when you really want to impress your guests.

INGREDIENTS:

4 cups of fresh red raspberries (pre-thawed if frozen), rinsed and patted dry

1 cup of white sugar

2 tablespoons of dried, edible lavender flowers

2 ½ cups of half and half

6 large egg yolks (separated from the whites)

¼ cup of fat free powdered milk

1 cup of heavy cream

2 teaspoons of pure vanilla extract

INSTRUCTIONS:

1. Make sure your freezer is set at or below 0 degrees Fahrenheit (-18 degrees Celsius). Place the ice cream bowl attachment in the freezer for at least 15 hours.

2. Check that the ice cream bowl is completely frozen by giving it a shake before use. If you hear no movement, the bowl's cooling liquid is properly frozen.

3. In a food processor or blender, puree the raspberries until thoroughly smooth.

4. Strain the raspberry puree through a fine mesh sieve, then discard the seeds and keep the approximately 2 cups that will have strained through.

5. In a saucepan at least 2 ½ quarts in capacity, place the sugar and 1 ¼ cups of the half and half to simmer over a medium heat. Stir continuously and, once the sugar is fully dissolved, adjust the heat to low to keep the mixture warm.

6. Using your stand mixer and a mixing bowl, whisk or whip the egg yolks for approximately 2 minutes until they're thickened.

7. While whisking the egg yolks, add in ½ cup of the hot half and half and sugar mixture, and whisk thoroughly until all ingredients are completely combined.

8. Pour the mixture with the egg yolks into the saucepan with the rest of the warm half and half and sugar, and raise the heat under the saucepan back up to medium.

9. Continuously stir the mixture in the saucepan with a wooden spoon, until it has thickened to a custard-like consistency.

10. Stir in the remaining half and half, the powdered milk, the heavy cream, and the dried edible lavender.

11. Continue to stir for a few more minutes, then remove the saucepan from the heat and strain the mixture through a fine mesh strainer into a large mixing bowl.

12. Stir in the reserved raspberry puree and vanilla extract, then cover the mixing bowl and refrigerate for at least 6 hours.

13. Take the ice cream freezer bowl out of the freezer and set it on the middle of your stand mixer's base.

14. Slide the assembly drive onto the bottom of the mixer head. Fit the dasher into the bowl and connect to the assembly drive.

15. When your stand mixer is prepared, switch it into "Level 1" or "Stir" mode. The dasher will begin to turn in the bowl. Pour the refrigerated mixture immediately from the mixing bowl into the freezer bowl.

16. After approximately 25-30 minutes, the mixture will have frozen to a thick, creamy soft-serve consistency. Serve directly from the ice cream freezer bowl into serving bowls or cones, and enjoy!

17. For a more hard-frozen consistency, transfer the mixture from the freezer bowl into an air-tight container and keep in the freezer for at least 2 more hours.

LILY CHARLES

Green Tea Gelato

Looking for a dessert that's both uplifting and a tad healthy? There's no better option than this awesome green tea gelato, which combines the focus friendly energy boost of the tea with all the creamy goodness of a well made gelato. This recipe is surprisingly easy, with a good freezing appliance, yet feels very sophisticated.

INGREDIENTS:

3 ¼ cups of whole milk

8 green tea bags

1 cup of white sugar

1 cup of heavy cream

8 large egg yolks (separated from the whites)

¼ cup of fat free powdered milk

INSTRUCTIONS:

1. Make sure your freezer is set at or below 0 degrees Fahrenheit (-18 degrees Celsius). Place the ice cream bowl attachment in the freezer for at least 15 hours.

2. Check that the ice cream bowl is completely frozen by giving it a shake before use. If you hear no movement, the bowl's cooling liquid is properly frozen.

3. Pour the milk into a saucepan and heat until it's at a low simmer.

4. In a medium sized bowl, pour half of the warmed milk over the tea bags, and set to steep for 30 minutes.

5. After 30 minutes, strain the bowl with the tea bags, and squeeze out all the liquid from the tea bags.

6. Pour the powdered milk into the milk that remains in the saucepan, and stir gently over a low heat.

7. Using your stand mixer and a mixing bowl, whisk the egg yolks and the sugar, until evenly combined and thickened.

8. Pour the egg and sugar mixture back into the saucepan, and thoroughly stir together with the warming milk.

9. Add the tea-infused milk into the saucepan, and raise the heat to medium. Stir the mixture continuously with a wooden spoon, until the mixture has reached a custard-like consistency.

10. Strain the custard from the saucepan into a medium sized bowl.

11. Stir in the cream until thoroughly combined, then cover and refrigerate for at least 6 hours.

12. Take the ice cream freezer bowl out of the freezer and set it on the middle of your stand mixer's base.

13. Slide the assembly drive onto the bottom of the mixer head. Fit the dasher into the bowl and connect to the assembly drive.

14. When your stand mixer is prepared, switch it into "Level 1" or "Stir" mode. The dasher will begin to turn in the bowl. Pour the refrigerated mixture immediately from the mixing bowl into the freezer bowl.

15. After approximately 25-30 minutes, the mixture will have frozen to a thick, creamy soft-serve consistency. Serve directly from the ice cream freezer bowl into serving bowls or cones, and enjoy!

BLUEBERRY CASSIS GELATO

This gelato is as beautiful as it is tasty to eat. The crème de cassis is a dark red liqueur made from the black currant. The recipe packs plenty of berry favor and a bold, beautiful coloring. This gelato will be a refreshing treat after any meal, or simply the perfect snack when you're looking for something sweet with a fruity twist.

INGREDIENTS:

5 cups of fresh blueberries (pre-thawed if frozen), rinsed and patted dry

¼ cup of crème de cassis, divided

1 cup of white sugar

1 cup of whole milk

2 ½ cups of half and half, divided

6 large egg yolks (separated from the whites)

½ cup of fat free powdered milk

1 cup of heavy cream

2 teaspoons of pure vanilla extract

INSTRUCTIONS:

1. Make sure your freezer is set at or below 0 degrees Fahrenheit (-18 degrees Celsius). Place the ice cream bowl attachment in the freezer for at least 15 hours.

2. Check that the ice cream bowl is completely frozen by giving it a shake before use. If you hear no movement, the bowl's cooling liquid is properly frozen.

3. In a food processor or blender, puree the blueberries until thoroughly smooth.

4. Strain the blueberry puree through a fine mesh sieve, then discard the seeds and skins, and keep the approximately 3 cups of blueberry puree that will have strained through.

5. In a large saucepan, combine the blueberry puree with 3 tablespoons of the crème de cassis, and stir continuously over a low to medium heat.

6. Once the mixture is reduced by half, pour it from the saucepan into a mixing bowl, cover and refrigerate.

7. Rinse out the saucepan and re-use to combine the sugar and 1 ½ cups of the half and half to simmer over a medium heat. Stir continuously and, once the sugar is fully dissolved, adjust the heat to low to keep the mixture warm.

8. Using your stand mixer and a mixing bowl, whisk or whip the egg yolks for approximately 2 minutes until they're thickened.

9. While whisking the egg yolks, add in ½ cup of the hot half and half and sugar mixture, and whisk thoroughly until all ingredients are completely combined.

10. Pour the mixture with the egg yolks into the saucepan with the rest of the warm half and half and sugar, and raise the heat under the saucepan back up to medium.

11. Continuously stir the mixture in the saucepan with a wooden spoon, until it has thickened to a custard-like consistency.

12. Stir in the remaining half and half, the powdered milk, the heavy cream, and the whole milk.

13. Continue to stir for a few more minutes, then remove the saucepan from the heat and strain the mixture through a fine mesh strainer into a large mixing bowl.

14. Stir in the reserved blueberry puree, the vanilla extract, and the remaining crème de cassis, then cover the mixing bowl and refrigerate for at least 6 hours.

15. Take the ice cream freezer bowl out of the freezer and set it on the middle of your stand mixer's base.

16. Slide the assembly drive onto the bottom of the mixer head. Fit the dasher into the bowl and connect to the assembly drive.

17. When your stand mixer is prepared, switch it into "Level 1" or "Stir" mode. The dasher will begin to turn in the bowl. Pour the refrigerated mixture immediately from the mixing bowl into the freezer bowl.

18. After approximately 25-30 minutes, the mixture will have frozen to a thick, creamy soft-serve consistency. Serve directly from the ice cream freezer bowl into serving bowls or cones, and enjoy!

19. For a more hard-frozen consistency, transfer the mixture from the freezer bowl into an air-tight container and keep in the freezer for at least 2 more hours.

LILY CHARLES

Chocolate Hazelnut Gelato

Get ready for a true indulgence! The dessert flavor power duo of chocolate and hazelnut comes together in perfect harmony in this awesome gelato, bolstered with crushed hazelnuts and swirls of hazelnut-laced chocolate sauce. I'll be the first to admit that it's not the healthiest dessert in the world, but it is definitely one of the most delicious!

INGREDIENTS:

3 cups of coarsely chopped shelled hazelnuts

½ cup of white sugar

1 cup of Nutella spread (or any other chocolate hazelnut spread will do)

1 cup of semisweet chocolate, coarsely chopped

1 cup of whole milk

2 cups of half and half, divided

6 large egg yolks (separated from the whites)

1 ½ cups of heavy cream

1 teaspoon of almond extract

INSTRUCTIONS:

1. Make sure your freezer is set at or below 0 degrees Fahrenheit (-18 degrees Celsius). Place the ice cream bowl attachment in the freezer for at least 15 hours.

2. Check that the ice cream bowl is completely frozen by giving it a shake before use. If you hear no movement, the bowl's cooling liquid is properly frozen.

3. In a large saucepan, combine the semisweet chocolate with ¾ cup of the heavy cream, and stir continuously over a low to medium heat until the chocolate melts and has blended completely with the cream.

4. Once the mixture is blended, pour it from the saucepan into a mixing bowl, cover and refrigerate.

5. Rinse out the saucepan and re-use to combine the sugar and 1 ½ cups of the half and half milk to simmer over a medium heat. Stir continuously and, once the sugar is fully dissolved, adjust the heat to low to keep the mixture warm.

6. Using your stand mixer and a mixing bowl, whisk or whip the egg yolks for approximately 2 minutes until they're thickened.

7. While whisking the egg yolks, add in ½ cup of the hot half and half and sugar mixture, and whisk thoroughly until all ingredients are completely combined.

8. Pour the mixture with the egg yolks into the saucepan with the rest of the warm half and half and sugar, and raise the heat under the saucepan back up to medium.

9. Continuously stir the mixture in the saucepan with a wooden spoon, until it has thickened to a custard-like consistency.

10. Stir in the remaining half and half, the powdered milk, and the whole milk.

11. Continue to stir for a few more minutes, then remove the saucepan from the heat and strain the mixture through a fine mesh strainer into a large mixing bowl.

12. Stir in the vanilla extract and the remaining heavy cream, then cover the mixing bowl and refrigerate for at least 6 hours.

13. Take the ice cream freezer bowl out of the freezer and set it on the middle of your stand mixer's base.

14. Slide the assembly drive onto the bottom of the mixer head. Fit the dasher into the bowl and connect to the assembly drive.

15. When your stand mixer is prepared, switch it into "Level 1" or "Stir" mode. The dasher will begin to turn in the bowl. Pour the refrigerated mixture immediately from the mixing bowl into the freezer bowl.

16. After approximately 20 minutes, pour the nutella/chocolate hazelnut spread directly into the freezer bowl, along with the chopped hazelnuts and continue freezing for another 5 minutes.

17. After approximately 25-30 minutes (total), the mixture will have frozen to a thick, creamy soft-serve consistency, laced through with the chocolate and hazelnut spread and nuts. Serve directly from the ice cream freezer bowl into serving bowls or cones, and enjoy!

18. For a more hard-frozen consistency, transfer the mixture from the freezer bowl into an air-tight container and keep in the freezer for at least 2 more hours.

LILY CHARLES

MARVELOUS MANGO GELATO

Mango has to be my absolute all time favorite fruit flavor. There's just nothing quite so luxurious as that sweet, tropical taste. This amazing recipe for mango gelato perfectly showcases that flavor, in a smooth, creamy, refreshing frozen confection that is surprisingly easy to prepare.

INGREDIENTS:

1 ½ pounds of 1-inch fresh mango cubes (thawed, if frozen)

½ cup of mango nectar

2 cups of whole milk

1 cup of white sugar

¼ cup of fat free powdered milk

1 cup of light cream

8 large egg yolks (separated from the whites)

1 teaspoon of pure vanilla extract

INSTRUCTIONS:

1. Make sure your freezer is set at or below 0 degrees Fahrenheit (-18 degrees Celsius). Place the ice cream bowl attachment in the freezer for at least 15 hours.

2. Check that the ice cream bowl is completely frozen by giving it a shake before use. If you hear no movement, the bowl's cooling liquid is properly frozen.

3. In a food processor or blender, puree the mango cubes until thoroughly smooth.

4. Strain the mango puree through a fine mesh sieve, discarding the pulp, and keep the approximately 2 ½ cups of mango puree that will have strained through.
5. Stir the mango nectar in with the strained puree, combine thoroughly, then cover and refrigerate for at least 30 minutes.
6. In a large saucepan, combine the milk, sugar, and powdered milk, bringing to simmer over a medium heat. Stir continuously and, once the sugar is fully dissolved, adjust the heat to low to keep the mixture warm.
7. Using your stand mixer and a mixing bowl, whisk or whip the egg yolks for approximately 2 minutes until they're thickened.
8. While whisking the egg yolks, slowly stir in 1 cup of the sugar and hot milk mixture from the saucepan, and whisk thoroughly until all ingredients are completely combined.
9. Pour the mixture with the egg yolks back into the saucepan with the rest of the milk and sugar, and raise the heat under the saucepan back up to medium.
10. Continuously stir the mixture in the saucepan with a wooden spoon, until it has thickened to a custard-like consistency.
11. Continue to stir for a few more minutes, then remove the saucepan from the heat and strain the custard-like mixture through a fine mesh strainer into a large mixing bowl.
12. Stir the reserved mango puree, the cream and the vanilla extract and mix until all ingredients are fully combined.
13. Cover the mixing bowl and refrigerate for at least 6 hours.
14. Take the ice cream freezer bowl out of the freezer and set it on the middle of your stand mixer's base.
15. Slide the assembly drive onto the bottom of the mixer head. Fit the dasher into the bowl and connect to the assembly drive.
16. When your stand mixer is prepared, switch it into "Level 1" or "Stir" mode. The dasher will begin to turn in the bowl. Pour the

refrigerated mixture immediately from the mixing bowl into the freezer bowl.

17. After approximately 25-30 minutes, the mixture will have frozen to a thick, creamy soft-serve consistency. Serve directly from the ice cream freezer bowl into serving bowls or cones, and enjoy!

18. For a more hard-frozen consistency, transfer the mixture from the freezer bowl into an air-tight container and keep in the freezer for at least 2 more hours.

LILY CHARLES

BLACKBERRY CREAM GELATO

Bursting with flavor, ripe and juicy, just the right mix of sweet and sour, blackberries have a flavor all their own. This blackberry cream gelato is the perfect preparation for that flavor sensation, a dense, creamy custard base,,loaded with beautiful blackberries. A dollop of whipped cream and a few fresh blackberries are the perfect toppers to this luscious gelato.

INGREDIENTS:

5 cups of fresh blackberries (pre-thawed if frozen), rinsed and patted dry

1 cup of white sugar

1 cup of whole milk

3 cups of half and half, divided

6 large egg yolks (separated from the whites)

½ cup of fat free powdered milk

1 ½ cups of heavy cream

2 teaspoons of pure vanilla extract

INSTRUCTIONS:

1. Make sure your freezer is set at or below 0 degrees Fahrenheit (-18 degrees Celsius). Place the ice cream bowl attachment in the freezer for at least 15 hours.

2. Check that the ice cream bowl is completely frozen by giving it a shake before use. If you hear no movement, the bowl's cooling liquid is properly frozen.

3. In a food processor or blender, puree the blackberries until thoroughly smooth.

4. Strain the blackberry puree through a fine mesh sieve, then discard the seeds and skins, and keep the approximately 3 cups of blackberry puree that will have strained through.
5. In a large saucepan, combine the blackberry puree with ¾ cup of the heavy cream, and stir continuously over a low to medium heat.
6. Once the mixture is reduced by half, pour it from the saucepan into a mixing bowl, cover and refrigerate.
7. Rinse out the saucepan and re-use to combine the sugar and 1 ½ cups of the half and half to simmer over a medium heat. Stir continuously and, once the sugar is fully dissolved, adjust the heat to low to keep the mixture warm.
8. Using your stand mixer and a mixing bowl, whisk or whip the egg yolks for approximately 2 minutes until they're thickened.
9. While whisking the egg yolks, add in ½ cup of the hot half and half and sugar mixture, and whisk thoroughly until all ingredients are completely combined.
10. Pour the mixture with the egg yolks into the saucepan with the rest of the warm half and half and sugar, and raise the heat under the saucepan back up to medium.
11. Continuously stir the mixture in the saucepan with a wooden spoon, until it has thickened to a custard-like consistency.
12. Stir in the remaining half and half, the powdered milk, and the whole milk.
13. Continue to stir for a few more minutes, then remove the saucepan from the heat and strain the mixture through a fine mesh strainer into a large mixing bowl.
14. Stir in the reserved blackberry puree, the vanilla extract, and the remaining heavy cream, then cover the mixing bowl and refrigerate for at least 6 hours.
15. Take the ice cream freezer bowl out of the freezer and set it on the middle of your stand mixer's base.

KitchenAid® Ice Cream

16. Slide the assembly drive onto the bottom of the mixer head. Fit the dasher into the bowl and connect to the assembly drive.

17. When your stand mixer is prepared, switch it into "Level 1" or "Stir" mode. The dasher will begin to turn in the bowl. Pour the refrigerated mixture immediately from the mixing bowl into the freezer bowl.

18. After approximately 25-30 minutes, the mixture will have frozen to a thick, creamy soft-serve consistency. Serve directly from the ice cream freezer bowl into serving bowls or cones, and enjoy!

19. For a more hard-frozen consistency, transfer the mixture from the freezer bowl into an air-tight container and keep in the freezer for at least 2 more hours.

LEMONADE GELATO

Who doesn't love a tall, crisp, refreshing glass of lemonade? There is nothing quite so tasty – except, perhaps, that same tall, crisp, refreshing glass of lemonade frozen into a creamy, dense, decadent gelato. This recipe is so simple – simply irresistible, that is – and I know your family will love it as much as mine does.

INGREDIENTS:

1 cup of unsweetened lemon juice (fresh or frozen from concentrate and thawed is fine)

2 cups of whole milk

1 ¾ cups of white sugar

¼ cup of fat free powdered milk

1 cup of light cream

8 large egg yolks (separated from the whites)

INSTRUCTIONS:

1. Make sure your freezer is set at or below 0 degrees Fahrenheit (-18 degrees Celsius). Place the ice cream bowl attachment in the freezer for at least 15 hours.

2. Check that the ice cream bowl is completely frozen by giving it a shake before use. If you hear no movement, the bowl's cooling liquid is properly frozen.

3. In a large saucepan, combine the milk, sugar, and powdered milk, bringing to simmer over a medium heat. Stir continuously and, once the sugar is fully dissolved, adjust the heat to low to keep the mixture warm.

4. Using your stand mixer and a mixing bowl, whisk or whip the egg yolks for approximately 2 minutes until they're thickened.
5. While whisking the egg yolks, slowly stir in 1 cup of the sugar and hot milk mixture from the saucepan, and whisk thoroughly until all ingredients are completely combined.
6. Pour the mixture with the egg yolks into the saucepan with the rest of the milk and sugar, and raise the heat under the saucepan back up to medium.
7. Continuously stir the mixture in the saucepan with a wooden spoon, until it has thickened to a custard-like consistency.
8. Continue to stir for a few more minutes, then remove the saucepan from the heat and strain the custard-like mixture through a fine mesh strainer into a large mixing bowl.
9. Stir in the lemon juice and the light cream, and mix until all ingredients are fully combined.
10. Cover the mixing bowl and refrigerate for at least 6 hours.
11. Take the ice cream freezer bowl out of the freezer and set it on the middle of your stand mixer's base.
12. Slide the assembly drive onto the bottom of the mixer head. Fit the dasher into the bowl and connect to the assembly drive.
13. When your stand mixer is prepared, switch it into "Level 1" or "Stir" mode. The dasher will begin to turn in the bowl. Pour the refrigerated mixture immediately from the mixing bowl into the freezer bowl.
14. After approximately 25-30 minutes, the mixture will have frozen to a thick, creamy soft-serve consistency. Serve directly from the ice cream freezer bowl into serving bowls or cones, and enjoy!
15. For a more hard-frozen consistency, transfer the mixture from the freezer bowl into an air-tight container and keep in the freezer for at least 2 more hours.

Cinnamon Spice Autumn Gelato

The flavor combo in this silky smooth gelato contains all my favorites of the fall, sweet cinnamon, spicy nutmeg, and a hint of cloves. Each bite boasts the rich, spicy taste of autumn and it is as aromatic as you'd imagine! Enjoy this gelato year-around and be sure to have some in your freezer when fall rolls around!

INGREDIENTS:

2 ½ teaspoons of ground cinnamon

1 ½ teaspoons of ground nutmeg

½ teaspoon of ground cloves

1 cup of white sugar

2 ½ cups of half and half

6 large egg yolks (separated from the whites)

¼ cup of fat free powdered milk

1 cup of heavy cream

1 teaspoon of pure vanilla extract

INSTRUCTIONS:

1. Make sure your freezer is set at or below 0 degrees Fahrenheit (-18 degrees Celsius). Place the ice cream bowl attachment in the freezer for at least 15 hours.

2. Check that the ice cream bowl is completely frozen by giving it a shake before use. If you hear no movement, the bowl's cooling liquid is properly frozen.

3. In a saucepan at least 2 ½ quarts in capacity, place the sugar and 1 ¼ cups of the half and half to simmer over a medium heat. Stir continuously and, once the sugar is fully dissolved, adjust the heat to low to keep the mixture warm.

4. Using your stand mixer and a mixing bowl, whisk or whip the egg yolks for approximately 2 minutes until they're thickened.

5. While whisking the egg yolks, add in ½ cup of the hot half and half and sugar mixture, and whisk thoroughly until all ingredients are completely combined.

6. Pour the mixture with the egg yolks into the saucepan with the rest of the warm half and half and sugar, and raise the heat under the saucepan back up to medium.

7. Continuously stir the mixture in the saucepan with a wooden spoon, until it has thickened to a custard-like consistency.

8. Stir in the remaining half and half and the powdered milk, and continue to stir for a few more minutes.

9. Remove the saucepan from the heat and strain the mixture through a fine mesh strainer into a large mixing bowl.

10. Stir in the cream, cinnamon, nutmeg, cloves, and vanilla extract, then cover the mixing bowl and refrigerate for at least 6 hours.

11. Take the ice cream freezer bowl out of the freezer and set it on the middle of your stand mixer's base.

12. Slide the assembly drive onto the bottom of the mixer head. Fit the dasher into the bowl and connect to the assembly drive.

13. When your stand mixer is prepared, switch it into "Level 1" or "Stir" mode. The dasher will begin to turn in the bowl. Pour the refrigerated mixture immediately from the mixing bowl into the freezer bowl.

14. After approximately 25-30 minutes, the mixture will have frozen to a thick, creamy soft-serve consistency. Serve directly from the ice cream freezer bowl into serving bowls or cones, and enjoy!

Passion Fruit Nectar Gelato

There is nothing quite like the sweet exotic flavor of the passion fruit. This rich passion fruit infused gelato is the ideal showcase for that most special of flavors and best of all, it's surprisingly simple to prepare. Get ready to prepare a perfect frozen tropical treat!

INGREDIENTS:

1 ½ cups of strained passion fruit juice (fresh or frozen from concentrate and thawed, as long as it's unsweetened)

1 teaspoon of concentrated passion fruit nectar

2 cups of whole milk

1 cup of white sugar

¼ cup of fat free powdered milk

1 cup of light cream

8 large egg yolks (separated from the whites)

INSTRUCTIONS:

1. Make sure your freezer is set at or below 0 degrees Fahrenheit (-18 degrees Celsius). Place the ice cream bowl attachment in the freezer for at least 15 hours.

2. Check that the ice cream bowl is completely frozen by giving it a shake before use. If you hear no movement, the bowl's cooling liquid is properly frozen.

3. In a large saucepan, combine the milk, sugar, and powdered milk, bringing to simmer over a medium heat. Stir continuously and, once the sugar is fully dissolved, adjust the heat to low to keep the mixture warm.

4. Using your stand mixer and a mixing bowl, whisk or whip the egg yolks for approximately 2 minutes until they're thickened.

5. While whisking the egg yolks, slowly stir in 1 cup of the sugar and hot milk mixture from the saucepan, and whisk thoroughly until all ingredients are completely combined.

6. Pour the mixture with the egg yolks into the saucepan with the rest of the warm milk and sugar, and raise the heat under the saucepan back up to medium.

7. Continuously stir the mixture in the saucepan with a wooden spoon, until it has thickened to a custard-like consistency.

8. Continue to stir for a few more minutes, then remove the saucepan from the heat and strain the custard-like mixture through a fine mesh strainer into a large mixing bowl.

9. Stir in the passion fruit juice, the passion fruit nectar and the light cream, and mix until all ingredients are fully combined.

10. Cover the mixing bowl and refrigerate for at least 6 hours.

11. Take the ice cream freezer bowl out of the freezer and set it on the middle of your stand mixer's base.

12. Slide the assembly drive onto the bottom of the mixer head. Fit the dasher into the bowl and connect to the assembly drive.

13. When your stand mixer is prepared, switch it into "Level 1" or "Stir" mode. The dasher will begin to turn in the bowl. Pour the refrigerated mixture immediately from the mixing bowl into the freezer bowl.

14. After approximately 25-30 minutes, the mixture will have frozen to a thick, creamy soft-serve consistency. Serve directly from the ice cream freezer bowl into serving bowls or cones, and enjoy!

15. For a more hard-frozen consistency, transfer the mixture from the freezer bowl into an air-tight container and keep in the freezer for at least 2 more hours.

Rosehip Tea Gelato

If you want a dessert that's as sweet on the spirit as it is on the tastebuds, look no further than this fantastic rosehip tea gelato. This recipe combines the antioxidant rich and immune boosting properties of rosehip tea with all the indulgent dense deliciousness of well made gelato. This is a gelato to feel good about eating!

INGREDIENTS:

3 ¼ cups of whole milk
8 rosehip tea bags
1 cup of white sugar
1 cup of heavy cream
8 large egg yolks (separated from the whites)
¼ cup of fat free powdered milk

INSTRUCTIONS:

1. Make sure your freezer is set at or below 0 degrees Fahrenheit (-18 degrees Celsius). Place the ice cream bowl attachment in the freezer for at least 15 hours.

2. Check that the ice cream bowl is completely frozen by giving it a shake before use. If you hear no movement, the bowl's cooling liquid is properly frozen.

3. Pour the milk into a saucepan and heat until it's at a low simmer.

4. In a medium sized bowl, pour half of the warmed milk over the tea bags, and set to steep for 30 minutes.

5. After 30 minutes, strain the bowl with the tea bags, and squeeze out all the liquid from the tea bags.
6. Pour the powdered milk into the milk that remains in the saucepan, and stir gently over a low heat.
7. Using your stand mixer and a mixing bowl, whisk the egg yolks and the sugar, until evenly combined and thickened.
8. Pour the egg and sugar mixture back into the saucepan, and thoroughly stir together with the warming milk.
9. Add the tea-infused milk into the saucepan, and raise the heat to medium. Stir the mixture continuously with a wooden spoon, until the mixture has reached a custard-like consistency.
10. Strain the custard from the saucepan into a medium sized bowl.
11. Stir in the cream until thoroughly combined, then cover and refrigerate for at least 6 hours.
12. Take the ice cream freezer bowl out of the freezer and set it on the middle of your stand mixer's base.
13. Slide the assembly drive onto the bottom of the mixer head. Fit the dasher into the bowl and connect to the assembly drive.
14. When your stand mixer is prepared, switch it into "Level 1" or "Stir" mode. The dasher will begin to turn in the bowl. Pour the refrigerated mixture immediately from the mixing bowl into the freezer bowl.
15. After approximately 25-30 minutes, the mixture will have frozen to a thick, creamy soft-serve consistency. Serve directly from the ice cream freezer bowl into serving bowls or cones, and enjoy!
16. For a more hard-frozen consistency, transfer the mixture from the freezer bowl into an air-tight container and keep in the freezer for at least 2 more hours.

BOYSENBERRY CREAM GELATO

If you can find boysenberries at the market – fresh or frozen – snap them up immediately and head to your kitchen to whip up this incredibly yummy gelato. The boysenberry taste is somewhere between the sweetness of raspberries and the tartness of blackberries, for a sweet and tangy flavor all its own. This boysenberry infused gelato perfectly highlights that unique flavor with dense creamy frozen custard, for a dessert that is as delicious as it is unique.

INGREDIENTS:

3 cups of chopped boysenberries, rinsed and patted dry (or thawed and drained of excess liquid, if frozen)

2 cups of whole milk

1 ¾ cups of white sugar

¼ cup of fat free powdered milk

1 cup of light cream

8 large egg yolks (separated from the whites)

INSTRUCTIONS:

1. Make sure your freezer is set at or below 0 degrees Fahrenheit (-18 degrees Celsius). Place the ice cream bowl attachment in the freezer for at least 15 hours.

2. Check that the ice cream bowl is completely frozen by giving it a shake before use. If you hear no movement, the bowl's cooling liquid is properly frozen.

3. In a large saucepan, combine the milk, sugar, boysenberries, and powdered milk, bringing to simmer over a medium heat. Stir continuously and, once the sugar is fully dissolved, adjust the heat to low to keep the mixture warm.

4. Using your stand mixer and a mixing bowl, whisk or whip the egg yolks for approximately 2 minutes until they're thickened.

5. While whisking the egg yolks, slowly stir in 1 cup of the heated mixture from the saucepan, and whisk thoroughly until all ingredients are completely combined. The boysenberries will remain chunky, which is fine.

6. Pour the mixture back into the saucepan with the rest, and raise the heat under the saucepan back up to medium.

7. Continuously stir the mixture in the saucepan with a wooden spoon, until it has thickened to a custard-like consistency. The boysenberries should be largely dissolved by now, which will give the mixture a rich color and a sweet and tart fragrance.

8. Continue to stir for a few more minutes, then remove the saucepan from the heat and strain the custard-like mixture through a fine mesh strainer into a large mixing bowl. Discard the boysenberry husks that will be caught by the strainer.

9. Stir in the cream, and mix until all ingredients are fully combined.

10. Cover the mixing bowl and refrigerate for at least 6 hours.

11. Take the ice cream freezer bowl out of the freezer and set it on the middle of your stand mixer's base.

12. Slide the assembly drive onto the bottom of the mixer head. Fit the dasher into the bowl and connect to the assembly drive.

13. When your stand mixer is prepared, switch it into "Level 1" or "Stir" mode. The dasher will begin to turn in the bowl. Pour the refrigerated mixture immediately from the mixing bowl into the freezer bowl.

14. After approximately 25-30 minutes, the mixture will have frozen to a thick, creamy soft-serve consistency. Serve directly from the ice cream freezer bowl into serving bowls or cones, and enjoy!

15. For a more hard-frozen consistency, transfer the mixture from the freezer bowl into an air-tight container and keep in the freezer for at least 2 more hours.

LILY CHARLES

FROZEN YOGURT

When frozen yogurt was first popularized in the American marketplace, the main reason to eat it instead of ice cream was because it has less fat and therefore will satisfy weight-conscious diet requirements. We've come a long way since then though those nutritional benefits to fro-yo hold as true as they ever have. These days, we've all rightly come to expect serious flavor and creamy consistency in our frozen yogurt, not "despite" its health benefits, but in addition to.

Frozen yogurt has thus come into its own, out from under the shadow of ice cream, able to be appreciated for its own unique rich flavor and luxurious consistency. Forget trying to buy or make frozen yogurt that "passes" as ice cream, and get excited about frozen yogurt because it's the perfect base for so many wonderful fruity, sweet, and even savory flavors! This section is filled with my favorite recipes for frozen yogurt that highlight its uniquely satisfying taste and consistency.

For kids and hungry adults alike, there is no better snack than peanut butter and banana fro-yo – both wholesome and delicious. Or perhaps you're looking to give a breakfast an extra kick? Try my awesome granola and raisin frozen yogurt. Trust me, there's a lot more to frozen yogurt than just being ice cream's low-fat counterpart. But don't take my word for it. Give these recipes a try, and see for yourself!

PINEAPPLE CHUNK FRO-YO

Pineapple is one of nature's greatest gifts, with every bite bursting with tropical flavors. This pineapple cream fro yo is the perfect way to get that vitamin packed pineapple infusion. This fro-yo will be a particularly welcome addition to your freezer in the cold dead of winter, when we could all use a little extra taste of sunshine!

INGREDIENTS:

3 cups of fresh ripe pineapples, rinsed and patted dry, peeled and diced into small chunks (frozen is fine, if thawed and drained of excess liquid)

1 ½ cups of whole milk

¾ cup of granulated sugar

1 cup of fresh pineapple juice (store bought is fine, as long as it's unsweetened)

3 cups of fat free vanilla yogurt

¼ cup of heavy cream

1 tablespoons of pure vanilla extract

INSTRUCTIONS:

1. Make sure your freezer is set at or below 0 degrees Fahrenheit (-18 degrees Celsius). Place the ice cream bowl attachment in the freezer for at least 15 hours.
2. Check that the ice cream bowl is completely frozen by giving it a shake before use. If you hear no movement, the bowl's cooling liquid is properly frozen.
3. In a mixing bowl, stir the pineapple chunks and ½ cup of the sugar.

4. Stir until pineapples are fully coated with the sugar, then leave to sit approximately two hours.

5. Using your stand mixer and a mixing bowl, stir the milk with the remaining sugar, until the sugar is fully dissolved.

6. Stir in the vanilla extract, the heavy cream, the yogurt, and the pineapple juice, stirring thoroughly until all ingredients are evenly combined. Cover and chill in the refrigerator for 1-2 hours.

7. Take the ice cream freezer bowl out of the freezer and set it on the middle of your stand mixer's base.

8. Slide the assembly drive onto the bottom of the mixer head. Fit the dasher into the bowl and connect to the assembly drive.

9. When your stand mixer is prepared, switch it into "Level 1" or "Stir" mode. The dasher will begin to turn in the bowl. Pour the refrigerated mixture immediately from the mixing bowl into the freezer bowl.

10. After approximately 20 minutes (in the last five minutes of freezing), add the sugar-coated pineapple chunks into the ice cream bowl to let mix completely and let freeze for another 5 minutes.

11. After approximately 25-30 minutes (total), the mixture will have frozen to a thick, creamy soft-serve consistency, with the frozen pineapple slices packed with melt in your mouth juicy goodness. Serve directly from the ice cream freezer bowl into serving bowls or cones, and enjoy!

12. For a more hard-frozen consistency, transfer the mixture from the freezer bowl into an air-tight container and keep in the freezer for at least 2 more hours.

Peanut Butter and Banana Fro-Yo

Remember peanut butter and banana sandwiches from childhood? They were one of my favorites - a balanced meal that tasted like a dessert. That's the inspiration behind this frozen yogurt recipe, which combines dense creamy peanut butter with delicious frozen banana chunks. Now that's a dessert that everyone can smile about.

INGREDIENTS:

2 ½ cups of peeled banana slices, cut to small bite sized chunks

1 ½ cups of whole milk

1 cup of smooth peanut butter, softened (any homemade or store bought preparation will do)

1 ½ cups of granulated sugar

3 cups of fat free vanilla yogurt

¼ cup of heavy cream

1 teaspoon of vanilla extract

INSTRUCTIONS:

1. Make sure your freezer is set at or below 0 degrees Fahrenheit (-18 degrees Celsius). Place the ice cream bowl attachment in the freezer for at least 15 hours.

2. Check that the ice cream bowl is completely frozen by giving it a shake before use. If you hear no movement, the bowl's cooling liquid is properly frozen.

3. Using your stand mixer and a mixing bowl, combine the milk with the sugar and the peanut butter until the sugar is fully dissolved and

the peanut butter and milk are evenly blended, approximately 4-5 minutes.

4. Stir in the vanilla extract, the heavy cream, and the yogurt, stirring thoroughly until all ingredients are evenly combined. Chill for 1-2 hours in the refrigerator.

5. Take the ice cream freezer bowl out of the freezer and set it on the middle of your stand mixer's base.

6. Slide the assembly drive onto the bottom of the mixer head. Fit the dasher into the bowl and connect to the assembly drive.

7. When your stand mixer is prepared, switch it into "Level 1" or "Stir" mode. The dasher will begin to turn in the bowl. Pour the refrigerated mixture immediately from the mixing bowl into the freezer bowl.

8. After approximately 20 minutes (in the last five minutes of freezing), add the banana chunks into the ice cream bowl to let mix completely. Let freeze for another 5 minutes.

9. After approximately 25-30 minutes (total), the mixture will have frozen to a thick, creamy soft-serve consistency, with the frozen banana chunks bursting sweet goodness throughout. Serve directly from the ice cream freezer bowl into serving bowls or cones, and enjoy!

10. For a more hard-frozen consistency, transfer the mixture from the freezer bowl into an air-tight container and keep in the freezer for at least 2 more hours.

WATERMELON FRO-YO

For my family, summertime is all about frozen treats and juicy, refreshing watermelon. So perhaps it's no surprise that my kids' favorite summer treat is my homemade watermelon frozen yogurt, which freezes watermelon goodness into a perfectly creamy frozen snack. The best part is how easy it is – the watermelon doesn't even require straining! What more could one ask from a refreshing frozen treat?

INGREDIENTS:

5 cups of fresh cubed watermelon, with the seeds removed

1 ½ cups of whole milk

¾ cups of granulated sugar

4 cups of fat free vanilla yogurt

¼ cup of heavy cream

1 tablespoons of pure vanilla extract

INSTRUCTIONS:

1. Make sure your freezer is set at or below 0 degrees Fahrenheit (-18 degrees Celsius). Place the ice cream bowl attachment in the freezer for at least 15 hours.

2. Check that the ice cream bowl is completely frozen by giving it a shake before use. If you hear no movement, the bowl's cooling liquid is properly frozen.

3. Using your stand mixer and a mixing bowl, combine the milk and sugar, at a low speed until the sugar is fully dissolved in the milk.

4. Stir in the yogurt, heavy cream, vanilla extract, and the watermelon cubes. Mash and whisk thoroughly until the watermelon and the other ingredients are fully combined. Place in the refrigerator for 1-2 hours.

5. Take the ice cream freezer bowl out of the freezer and set it on the middle of your stand mixer's base.

6. Slide the assembly drive onto the bottom of the mixer head. Fit the dasher into the bowl and connect to the assembly drive.

7. When your stand mixer is prepared, switch it into "Level 1" or "Stir" mode. The dasher will begin to turn in the bowl. Pour the refrigerated mixture immediately from the mixing bowl into the freezer bowl.

8. After approximately 25-30 minutes, the mixture will have frozen to a thick, creamy soft-serve consistency. Serve directly from the ice cream freezer bowl into serving bowls or cones, and enjoy!

9. For a more hard-frozen consistency, transfer the mixture from the freezer bowl into an air-tight container and keep in the freezer for at least 2 more hours.

VERY VANILLA FRO-YO

This recipe for classic vanilla frozen yogurt is a year round staple in our family. I usually have an airtight container of it in the icebox ready to go at any given time, as the perfect and relatively healthy base or side dish for near any dessert. Bonus points for dolloping a spoonful of this froyo with some fresh fruit over pancakes or waffles on weekends or for special occasion breakfasts!

INGREDIENTS:

1 2/3 cups of whole milk
¾ cup of granulated sugar
4 cups of fat free vanilla yogurt
¼ cup of heavy cream
1 tablespoons of pure vanilla extract
1 teaspoon of coarsely ground vanilla bean

INSTRUCTIONS:

1. Make sure your freezer is set at or below 0 degrees Fahrenheit (-18 degrees Celsius). Place the ice cream bowl attachment in the freezer for at least 15 hours.

2. Check that the ice cream bowl is completely frozen by giving it a shake before use. If you hear no movement, the bowl's cooling liquid is properly frozen.

3. Using your stand mixer and a mixing bowl, combine the milk and sugar, at a low speed until the sugar is fully dissolved in the milk.

4. Stir in the yogurt, heavy cream, vanilla extract, and ground vanilla bean. Cover and refrigerate for 1-2 hours.

5. Take the ice cream freezer bowl out of the freezer and set it on the middle of your stand mixer's base.

6. Slide the assembly drive onto the bottom of the mixer head. Fit the dasher into the bowl and connect to the assembly drive.

7. When your stand mixer is prepared, switch it into "Level 1" or "Stir" mode. The dasher will begin to turn in the bowl. Pour the refrigerated mixture immediately from the mixing bowl into the freezer bowl.

8. After approximately 25-30 minutes, the mixture will have frozen to a thick, creamy soft-serve consistency. Serve directly from the ice cream freezer bowl into serving bowls or cones, and enjoy!

9. For a more hard-frozen consistency, transfer the mixture from the freezer bowl into an air-tight container and keep in the freezer for at least 2 more hours.

ORANGE CREAM FRO-YO

The silky citrus blast that comes with every bite of this orange infused frozen yogurt is pure bliss. It's shockingly easy to make, and best of all it's incredibly healthy, since that sweet orange juice means a lot less sugar is going into this recipe than with most frozen yogurt.

INGREDIENTS:

1 ½ cups of whole milk

1 ½ cups of pulp free unsweetened orange juice (homemade or store bought is fine)

¼ cup of granulated sugar

3 cups of fat free vanilla yogurt

¼ cup of heavy cream

1 ½ teaspoons of vanilla extract

INSTRUCTIONS:

1. Make sure your freezer is set at or below 0 degrees Fahrenheit (-18 degrees Celsius). Place the ice cream bowl attachment in the freezer for at least 15 hours.
2. Check that the ice cream bowl is completely frozen by giving it a shake before use. If you hear no movement, the bowl's cooling liquid is properly frozen.
3. Using your stand mixer and a mixing bowl, combine the milk with the orange juice and sugar, at a low speed until the sugar is fully dissolved in the milk.
4. Stir in the yogurt, heavy cream and vanilla extract. Cover and refrigerate for 1-2 hours.

5. Take the ice cream freezer bowl out of the freezer and set it on the middle of your stand mixer's base.

6. Slide the assembly drive onto the bottom of the mixer head. Fit the dasher into the bowl and connect to the assembly drive.

7. When your stand mixer is prepared, switch it into "Level 1" or "Stir" mode. The dasher will begin to turn in the bowl. Pour the refrigerated mixture immediately from the mixing bowl into the freezer bowl.

8. After approximately 25-30 minutes, the mixture will have frozen to a thick, creamy soft-serve consistency. Serve directly from the ice cream freezer bowl into serving bowls or cones, and enjoy!

MINTY FRESH FRO-YO

If you like mint tea, you'll love this mint infused frozen yogurt that's both refreshing and calming. The mint gives a wonderful natural green hue to the fro-yo that kids will love, but the flavor itself will have everyone clamoring for a second scoop.

INGREDIENTS:

1 ½ cups of whole milk

1 ½ cups of unsweetened, cooled, steeped mint tea (steeped using between 7-10 mint-tea bags of the chef's choice)

1 ¼ cups of granulated sugar

3 cups of fat free vanilla yogurt

¼ cup of heavy cream

1 ½ teaspoons of vanilla extract

INSTRUCTIONS:

1. Make sure your freezer is set at or below 0 degrees Fahrenheit (-18 degrees Celsius). Place the ice cream bowl attachment in the freezer for at least 15 hours.

2. Check that the ice cream bowl is completely frozen by giving it a shake before use. If you hear no movement, the bowl's cooling liquid is properly frozen.

3. Using your stand mixer and a mixing bowl, combine the milk with the mint tea and sugar, at a low speed until the sugar is fully dissolved in the milk.

4. Stir in the yogurt, heavy cream and vanilla extract. Cover and refrigerate for 1-2 hours.

5. Take the ice cream freezer bowl out of the freezer and set it on the middle of your stand mixer's base.

6. Slide the assembly drive onto the bottom of the mixer head. Fit the dasher into the bowl and connect to the assembly drive.

7. When your stand mixer is prepared, switch it into "Level 1" or "Stir" mode. The dasher will begin to turn in the bowl. Pour the refrigerated mixture immediately from the mixing bowl into the freezer bowl.

8. After approximately 25-30 minutes, the mixture will have frozen to a thick, creamy soft-serve consistency. Serve directly from the ice cream freezer bowl into serving bowls or cones, and enjoy!

APPLE-PIE FRO-YO

This frozen yogurt is as American as apple pie and just as delicious. This recipe uses graham or ginger snap cookies crumbled into frozen chunks as your pie "crust" for true decadence in every bite. I always prefer to use chunky applesauce, because I like all the chunks I can get in my frozen yogurt, though smooth works just as well. Garnish with a dollop of whipped cream.

INGREDIENTS:

1 cup of packed brown sugar

2 tablespoons of molasses

1 ½ cups of whole milk

1 ¾ cups of unsweetened applesauce (homemade or store bought, chunky or smooth – chef's choice!)

2 ½ teaspoons of powdered cinnamon

3 ½ cups of low fat vanilla yogurt

1 teaspoon of pure vanilla extract

1 cup of crumbled gingersnaps or graham crackers

INSTRUCTIONS:

1. Make sure your freezer is set at or below 0 degrees Fahrenheit (-18 degrees Celsius). Place the ice cream bowl attachment in the freezer for at least 15 hours.

2. Check that the ice cream bowl is completely frozen by giving it a shake before use. If you hear no movement, the bowl's cooling liquid is properly frozen.

3. Using your stand mixer and a mixing bowl, combine the milk, brown sugar and molasses until the sugar is fully dissolved.

4. Stir in the applesauce, cinnamon, vanilla yogurt, and vanilla extract. Stir thoroughly until all ingredients are evenly blended. Cover and chill in the refrigerator for 1-2 hours.

5. Take the ice cream freezer bowl out of the freezer and set it on the middle of your stand mixer's base.

6. Slide the assembly drive onto the bottom of the mixer head. Fit the dasher into the bowl and connect to the assembly drive.

7. When your stand mixer is prepared, switch it into "Level 1" or "Stir" mode. The dasher will begin to turn in the bowl. Pour the refrigerated mixture immediately from the mixing bowl into the freezer bowl.

8. After approximately 20 minutes (in the last five minutes of freezing), add the crumbled graham crackers or gingersnap cookies into the freezer bowl to let mix completely. Let freeze for another 5 minutes.

9. After approximately 25-30 minutes (total), the mixture will have frozen to a thick, creamy soft-serve consistency, with the crumbled cookies perfectly frozen and embedded throughout. Serve directly from the ice cream freezer bowl into bowls or cones, and enjoy!

10. For a more hard-frozen consistency, transfer the mixture from the freezer bowl into an air-tight container and keep in the freezer for at least 2 more hours.

CARAMEL NUT CRUNCH FRO-YO

This frozen yogurt is a seriously fun treat, laced with caramel sauce and crushed walnuts, every bite is like a sweet flavor roller coaster. The classic sweetness of the caramel laden frozen yogurt is made even better by the texture of the walnuts. This fro-yo tastes great with any sort of topping you might add. Fudge sauce or even more caramel are often welcomed additions in our kitchen.

INGREDIENTS:

1 ½ cups of whole milk

1 cup of soft caramel sauce or syrup (any homemade or store bought preparation will do)

1 cup of coarsely chopped walnuts

1 ½ cups of granulated sugar

3 cups of fat free vanilla yogurt

¼ cup of heavy cream

1 ½ teaspoons of vanilla extract

INSTRUCTIONS:

1. Make sure your freezer is set at or below 0 degrees Fahrenheit (-18 degrees Celsius). Place the ice cream bowl attachment in the freezer for at least 15 hours.

2. Check that the ice cream bowl is completely frozen by giving it a shake before use. If you hear no movement, the bowl's cooling liquid is properly frozen.

3. Using your stand mixer and a mixing bowl, combine the milk with the sugar until the sugar is fully dissolved.

4. Stir in the vanilla extract, the heavy cream, and the yogurt, stirring thoroughly until all ingredients are evenly combined. Cover and refrigerate for 1-2 hours.

5. Take the ice cream freezer bowl out of the freezer and set it on the middle of your stand mixer's base.

6. Slide the assembly drive onto the bottom of the mixer head. Fit the dasher into the bowl and connect to the assembly drive.

7. When your stand mixer is prepared, switch it into "Level 1" or "Stir" mode. The dasher will begin to turn in the bowl. Pour the refrigerated mixture immediately from the mixing bowl into the freezer bowl.

8. After approximately 20 minutes (in the last five minutes of freezing), add the caramel sauce and the chopped nuts into the ice cream bowl to let mix completely. Let mix and freeze for another 5 minutes.

9. After approximately 25-30 minutes (total), the mixture will have frozen to a thick, creamy soft-serve consistency, with the caramel and nuts perfectly laced throughout every scoop. Serve directly from the ice cream freezer bowl into serving bowls or cones, and enjoy!

10. For a more hard-frozen consistency, transfer the mixture from the freezer bowl into an air-tight container and keep in the freezer for at least 2 more hours.

Pear Fro-Yo

If you happen to spot ripe pears at the market, grab them up and head for your freezing appliance, because this pear frozen yogurt is pure fruity bliss. There's just something about the simple sweetness of pears that works so perfectly in a frozen yogurt treat. My family loves this fro-yo, and I have no doubt yours will too.

INGREDIENTS:

5 cups of fresh ripe pears, cubed, peeled and mashed
1 ½ cups of whole milk
¾ cup of granulated sugar
4 cups of fat free vanilla yogurt
¼ cup of heavy cream
1 tablespoons of pure vanilla extract

INSTRUCTIONS:

1. Make sure your freezer is set at or below 0 degrees Fahrenheit (-18 degrees Celsius). Place the ice cream bowl attachment in the freezer for at least 15 hours.

2. Check that the ice cream bowl is completely frozen by giving it a shake before use. If you hear no movement, the bowl's cooling liquid is properly frozen.

3. Using your stand mixer and a mixing bowl, combine the milk and sugar, at a low speed until the sugar is fully dissolved in the milk.

4. Stir in the yogurt, heavy cream, vanilla extract, and the pear mash. Mash and whisk thoroughly until the pear and the other ingredients

are fully combined. It's fine if the pears remain a bit chunky – chef's choice! Cover and refrigerate for 1-2 hours.

5. Take the ice cream freezer bowl out of the freezer and set it on the middle of your stand mixer's base.

6. Slide the assembly drive onto the bottom of the mixer head. Fit the dasher into the bowl and connect to the assembly drive.

7. When your stand mixer is prepared, switch it into "Level 1" or "Stir" mode. The dasher will begin to turn in the bowl. Pour the refrigerated mixture immediately from the mixing bowl into the freezer bowl.

8. After approximately 25-30 minutes, the mixture will have frozen to a thick, creamy soft-serve consistency. Serve directly from the ice cream freezer bowl into serving bowls or cones, and enjoy!

9. For a more hard-frozen consistency, transfer the mixture from the freezer bowl into an air-tight container and keep in the freezer for at least 2 more hours.

TRIPLE CHOCOLATE FUDGE BROWNIE FRO-YO

Ok chocolate fiends, this one's for you. I won't try to pretend that this frozen yogurt is particularly healthy. Yes, it's yogurt instead of cream, but with chocolate yogurt, chocolate chips, and fudge brownie chunks, it's pretty hard to pretend this is a nutritious snack. Never mind though – it is 100% delicious, and entirely worth the calories – so go for it!

INGREDIENTS:

1 ½ cups of crumbled chocolate fudge brownies (your favorite home recipe or any store bought preparation will do, as long as they're cooled before using)

1 cup of semisweet dark chocolate chips

1 ½ cups of whole milk

1 cup of Dutch process cocoa powder

1 ½ cups of granulated sugar

3 cups of fat free vanilla yogurt

¼ cup of heavy cream

1 ½ teaspoons of vanilla extract

INSTRUCTIONS:

1. Make sure your freezer is set at or below 0 degrees Fahrenheit (-18 degrees Celsius). Place the ice cream bowl attachment in the freezer for at least 15 hours.

2. Check that the ice cream bowl is completely frozen by giving it a shake before use. If you hear no movement, the bowl's cooling liquid is properly frozen.

3. Using your stand mixer and a mixing bowl, combine the milk with the sugar and the Dutch process cocoa powder until all the ingredients are evenly blended.

4. Stir in the vanilla extract, the heavy cream, and the yogurt, stirring thoroughly until all ingredients are evenly blended. Cover and refrigerate for 1-2 hours.

5. Take the ice cream freezer bowl out of the freezer and set it on the middle of your stand mixer's base.

6. Slide the assembly drive onto the bottom of the mixer head. Fit the dasher into the bowl and connect to the assembly drive.

7. When your stand mixer is prepared, switch it into "Level 1" or "Stir" mode. The dasher will begin to turn in the bowl. Pour the refrigerated mixture immediately from the mixing bowl into the freezer bowl.

8. After approximately 20 minutes (in the last five minutes of freezing), add the crumbled brownie chunks and semi-sweet chocolate chips into the ice cream bowl to let mix completely.

9. After approximately 25-30 minutes (total), the mixture will have frozen to a thick, creamy soft-serve consistency, with the chocolate chips and brownie chunks perfectly frozen and embedded throughout. Serve directly from the ice cream freezer bowl into serving bowls or cones, and enjoy!

10. For a more hard-frozen consistency, transfer the mixture from the freezer bowl into an air-tight container and keep in the freezer for at least 2 more hours.

Berry Berry Fro-Yo

This berry packed tasty frozen yogurt is a fantastic way to get some fruit into your kids, and for adults, there's no sweeter means of keeping fruit in your diet year round. Feel free to play around with the amount of sugar in the recipe. This preparation keeps it on the low side, but those with a sweet tooth could increase the sugar to 1/3 cup and it tastes just dandy.

INGREDIENTS:

¾ cup of whole milk

¼ cup of granulated sugar

4 cups of low fat vanilla yogurt

18 ounces of frozen mixed berries (thawed, pureed and strained to remove seeds

1 tablespoon of pure lemon extract (or vanilla extract – chef's choice!)

INSTRUCTIONS:

1. Make sure your freezer is set at or below 0 degrees Fahrenheit (-18 degrees Celsius). Place the ice cream bowl attachment in the freezer for at least 15 hours.
2. Check that the ice cream bowl is completely frozen by giving it a shake before use. If you hear no movement, the bowl's cooling liquid is properly frozen.
3. Using your stand mixer and a mixing bowl, combine the milk and sugar, at a low speed until the sugar is fully dissolved in the milk.
4. Stir in the yogurt, berry puree and lemon (or vanilla) extract. Cover and refrigerate for 1-2 hours.

5. Take the ice cream freezer bowl out of the freezer and set it on the middle of your stand mixer's base.

6. Slide the assembly drive onto the bottom of the mixer head. Fit the dasher into the bowl and connect to the assembly drive.

7. When your stand mixer is prepared, switch it into "Level 1" or "Stir" mode. The dasher will begin to turn in the bowl. Pour the refrigerated mixture immediately from the mixing bowl into the freezer bowl.

8. After approximately 25-30 minutes, the mixture will have frozen to a thick, creamy soft-serve consistency. Serve directly from the ice cream freezer bowl into serving bowls or cones, and enjoy!

BLACK FOREST FRO-YO

This cherry and chocolate frozen yogurt is the perfect treat to have in your freezer when you want a dessert that tastes sinfully indulgent but isn't, really. I love the way this recipe perfectly captures the "Black Forest cake" magic of rich chocolate and luxurious maraschino cherries in every decadent frozen bite!

INGREDIENTS:

9 ounces of semisweet or bittersweet dark chocolate, divided into max. 1-inch pieces

1 ½ cups of whole milk

1/3 cup of granulated sugar

4 cups of low fat vanilla yogurt

¼ cup of maraschino cherry juice

1 cup of drained maraschino cherries, coarsely diced

INSTRUCTIONS:

1. Make sure your freezer is set at or below 0 degrees Fahrenheit (-18 degrees Celsius). Place the ice cream bowl attachment in the freezer for at least 15 hours.
2. Check that the ice cream bowl is completely frozen by giving it a shake before use. If you hear no movement, the bowl's cooling liquid is properly frozen.
3. In a medium sized saucepan, bring the milk up to simmer on a medium heat.
4. In a food processor or blender, pulse or chop the chocolate pieces.

5. While the processor or blender is running, pour the hot milk directly from the saucepan into the chocolate, and continue to process until the chocolate is melted.

6. Add the sugar, yogurt, and cherry juice to the milk and chocolate mixture, and continue to process until evenly combined and smooth.

7. Cover and refrigerate the mixture for at least two hours.

8. Take the ice cream freezer bowl out of the freezer and set it on the middle of your stand mixer's base.

9. Slide the assembly drive onto the bottom of the mixer head. Fit the dasher into the bowl and connect to the assembly drive.

10. When your stand mixer is prepared, switch it into "Level 1" or "Stir" mode. The dasher will begin to turn in the bowl. Pour the refrigerated mixture immediately from the mixing bowl into the freezer bowl.

11. In the last 5 minutes of freezing (after the mixture has been in the freezing appliance for approximately 20 minutes) add in the coarsely diced maraschino cherries into the freezer bowl to let mix completely.

12. After a total of 25-30 minutes, the mixture will have frozen to a thick, creamy soft-serve consistency. Serve directly from the ice cream freezer bowl into serving bowls or cones, and enjoy!

13. For a more hard-frozen consistency, transfer the mixture from the freezer bowl into an air-tight container and keep in the freezer for at least 2 more hours.

PLUM CINNAMON FRO-YO

The combination of sweet juicy plums and slightly spicy cinnamon is a sheer delight. These two distinct flavors marry perfectly in this chunky, creamy frozen yogurt, that's a delicious dessert or snack to serve up straight from the freezer any time of year.

INGREDIENTS:

3 cups of fresh ripe plums, rinsed, and patted dry (frozen is fine, if thawed and drained of excess liquid)

1 ½ cups of whole milk

1 ¼ cups of granulated sugar

1 ½ tablespoons of ground cinnamon

3 cups of fat free vanilla yogurt

¼ cup of heavy cream

½ tablespoon of pure vanilla extract

INSTRUCTIONS:

1. Make sure your freezer is set at or below 0 degrees Fahrenheit (-18 degrees Celsius). Place the ice cream bowl attachment in the freezer for at least 15 hours.
2. Check that the ice cream bowl is completely frozen by giving it a shake before use. If you hear no movement, the bowl's cooling liquid is properly frozen.
3. Peel and pit the plums, and slice into small chunks.
4. In a mixing bowl, stir the plums, the cinnamon, and ¾ cup of the sugar.

5. Stir until the sugar and cinnamon are dissolved and the plums are fully coated, then leave to sit approximately two hours.

6. Using your stand mixer and a mixing bowl, stir the milk with the remaining sugar until the sugar is fully dissolved.

7. Stir in the vanilla extract, the heavy cream and the yogurt, stirring thoroughly until all ingredients are evenly combined. Cover and chill in the refrigerator for 1-2 hours.

8. Take the ice cream freezer bowl out of the freezer and set it on the middle of your stand mixer's base.

9. Slide the assembly drive onto the bottom of the mixer head. Fit the dasher into the bowl and connect to the assembly drive.

10. When your stand mixer is prepared, switch it into "Level 1" or "Stir" mode. The dasher will begin to turn in the bowl. Pour the refrigerated mixture immediately from the mixing bowl into the freezer bowl.

11. After approximately 20 minutes (in the last five minutes of freezing), add the soaked plum chunks into the ice cream bowl to let mix completely.

12. After approximately 25-30 minutes (total), the mixture will have frozen to a thick, creamy soft-serve consistency, with the frozen plum chunks juicy and delicious throughout. Serve directly from the ice cream freezer bowl into serving bowls or cones, and enjoy!

13. For a more hard-frozen consistency, transfer the mixture from the freezer bowl into an air-tight container and keep in the freezer for at least 2 more hours.

RASPBERRY CHUNK FRO-YO

The cheery tart sweetness of raspberries is truly delicious – and nothing brings it out better than this rich, creamy frozen yogurt, with real raspberry chunks frozen in a swirl throughout. This is a wonderful anytime treat to have in your freezer for a dose of fruit and calcium that is as nutritious as it is delicious!

INGREDIENTS:

3 cups of fresh ripe raspberries, rinsed and patted dry (frozen is fine, if thawed and drained of excess liquid)

1 ½ cups of whole milk

1 ¼ cups of granulated sugar

1 cup of lemon juice (store bought is fine, as long as it's unsweetened)

3 cups of fat free vanilla yogurt

¼ cup of heavy cream

1 ½ tablespoons of pure vanilla extract

INSTRUCTIONS:

1. Make sure your freezer is set at or below 0 degrees Fahrenheit (-18 degrees Celsius). Place the ice cream bowl attachment in the freezer for at least 15 hours.
2. Check that the ice cream bowl is completely frozen by giving it a shake before use. If you hear no movement, the bowl's cooling liquid is properly frozen.
3. In a mixing bowl, stir the raspberries, the lemon juice, and ¾ cup of the sugar.
4. Stir until the sugar is dissolved and the raspberries are fully coated, then leave to sit approximately two hours.

5. Using your stand mixer and a mixing bowl, stir the milk with the remaining sugar until the sugar is fully dissolved.
6. Stir in the vanilla extract, the heavy cream and the yogurt, stirring thoroughly until all ingredients are evenly combined. Cover and refrigerate for 1-2 hours.
7. Take the ice cream freezer bowl out of the freezer and set it on the middle of your stand mixer's base.
8. Slide the assembly drive onto the bottom of the mixer head. Fit the dasher into the bowl and connect to the assembly drive.
9. When your stand mixer is prepared, switch it into "Level 1" or "Stir" mode. The dasher will begin to turn in the bowl. Pour the refrigerated mixture immediately from the mixing bowl into the freezer bowl.
10. After approximately 20 minutes (in the last five minutes of freezing), add the soaked raspberry chunks into the ice cream bowl to let mix completely.
11. After approximately 25-30 minutes (total), the mixture will have frozen to a thick, creamy soft-serve consistency, with the frozen raspberry chunks juicy and delicious throughout. Serve directly from the ice cream freezer bowl into serving bowls or cones, and enjoy!
12. For a more hard-frozen consistency, transfer the mixture from the freezer bowl into an air-tight container and keep in the freezer for at least 2 more hours.

GRANOLA AND RAISIN FRO-YO

This recipe is essentially a slightly sweeter, frozen version of that healthy breakfast classic – yogurt with crunchy granola, raisins, and just a drizzle of honey throughout. This is a favorite summer time breakfast in my household, though it is *definitely* tasty enough to serve as a dessert, as well!

INGREDIENTS:

1 ½ cups of whole milk

1 cup of crunchy crumbled granola (any homemade or store bought preparation will do – chef's choice!)

½ cup of sweet black or white raisins

½ cup of honey

¾ cups of granulated sugar

3 cups of fat free vanilla yogurt

¼ cup of heavy cream

1 ½ teaspoons of vanilla extract

INSTRUCTIONS:

1. Make sure your freezer is set at or below 0 degrees Fahrenheit (-18 degrees Celsius). Place the ice cream bowl attachment in the freezer for at least 15 hours.

2. Check that the ice cream bowl is completely frozen by giving it a shake before use. If you hear no movement, the bowl's cooling liquid is properly frozen.

3. Using your stand mixer and a mixing bowl, combine the milk with the sugar until the sugar is fully dissolved.

4. Stir in the vanilla extract, the heavy cream, and the yogurt, stirring thoroughly until all ingredients are evenly combined. Cover and refrigerate for 1-2 hours.

5. Take the ice cream freezer bowl out of the freezer and set it on the middle of your stand mixer's base.

6. Slide the assembly drive onto the bottom of the mixer head. Fit the dasher into the bowl and connect to the assembly drive.

7. When your stand mixer is prepared, switch it into "Level 1" or "Stir" mode. The dasher will begin to turn in the bowl. Pour the refrigerated mixture immediately from the mixing bowl into the freezer bowl.

8. After approximately 20 minutes (in the last five minutes of freezing), add the crumbled granola, the raisins, and the honey into the ice cream bowl to let mix completely.

9. After approximately 25-30 minutes (total), the mixture will have frozen to a thick, creamy soft-serve consistency, with the granola, raisins and honey laced throughout in delicious frozen ribbons. Serve directly from the ice cream freezer bowl into serving bowls or cones, and enjoy!

10. For a more hard-frozen consistency, transfer the mixture from the freezer bowl into an air-tight container and keep in the freezer for at least 2 more hours.

STRAWBERRY BANANA FRO-YO

Strawberries and bananas go together better than just about any fruit combo I can think of, so what better way to celebrate this classic duo than with this delicious fruit packed frozen yogurt? It couldn't be easier to prepare, and the result will be a delicious and nutritious cold confection for everyone!

INGREDIENTS:

1 ½ cups of whole milk

1 cup of ripe strawberries, with the stems discarded, rinsed, patted dry, and sliced into small pieces

1 cup of ripe bananas, peeled and sliced into bite sized pieces

1 ½ cups of granulated sugar

3 cups of fat free vanilla yogurt

¼ cup of heavy cream

1 ½ teaspoons of vanilla extract

INSTRUCTIONS:

1. Make sure your freezer is set at or below 0 degrees Fahrenheit (-18 degrees Celsius). Place the ice cream bowl attachment in the freezer for at least 15 hours.
2. Check that the ice cream bowl is completely frozen by giving it a shake before use. If you hear no movement, the bowl's cooling liquid is properly frozen.
3. Using your stand mixer and a mixing bowl, combine the milk with the sugar until the sugar is fully dissolved.

4. Stir in the vanilla extract, the heavy cream, and the yogurt, stirring thoroughly until all ingredients are evenly combined. Cover and chill in the refrigerator for 1-2 hours.

5. Take the ice cream freezer bowl out of the freezer and set it on the middle of your stand mixer's base.

6. Slide the assembly drive onto the bottom of the mixer head. Fit the dasher into the bowl and connect to the assembly drive.

7. When your stand mixer is prepared, switch it into "Level 1" or "Stir" mode. The dasher will begin to turn in the bowl. Pour the refrigerated mixture immediately from the mixing bowl into the freezer bowl.

8. After approximately 20 minutes (in the last five minutes of freezing), add the sliced bananas and strawberries into the ice cream bowl to let mix completely.

9. After approximately 25-30 minutes (total), the mixture will have frozen to a thick, creamy soft-serve consistency, with the fruit distributed in perfectly sweet chunks throughout. Serve directly from the ice cream freezer bowl into serving bowls or cones, and enjoy!

10. For a more hard-frozen consistency, transfer the mixture from the freezer bowl into an air-tight container and keep in the freezer for at least 2 more hours.

CARAMEL NOUGAT CHOCOLATE-SWIRL FRO-YO

If your mouth started to water from just reading the name of this recipe, you're not alone. This confection laden, chunky, swirled frozen yogurt treat is every bit as yummy as it sounds. This is a perfect preparation to have ready in your freezer for special occasions or for regular days when you just need a scoop of fun!

INGREDIENTS:

1 ½ cups of whole milk

¾ cup of soft candy nougat, sliced into small chunks approximately ¼-inch

¾ cup of caramel chips

¾ cup of chocolate syrup

1 ½ cups of granulated sugar

3 cups of fat free vanilla yogurt

¼ cup of heavy cream

1 ½ teaspoons of vanilla extract

INSTRUCTIONS:

1. Make sure your freezer is set at or below 0 degrees Fahrenheit (-18 degrees Celsius). Place the ice cream bowl attachment in the freezer for at least 15 hours.

2. Check that the ice cream bowl is completely frozen by giving it a shake before use. If you hear no movement, the bowl's cooling liquid is properly frozen.

3. Using your stand mixer and a mixing bowl, combine the milk with the sugar until the sugar is fully dissolved.

4. Stir in the vanilla extract, the heavy cream, and the yogurt, stirring thoroughly until all ingredients are evenly combined. Cover and refrigerate for 1-2 hours.

5. Take the ice cream freezer bowl out of the freezer and set it on the middle of your stand mixer's base.

6. Slide the assembly drive onto the bottom of the mixer head. Fit the dasher into the bowl and connect to the assembly drive.

7. When your stand mixer is prepared, switch it into "Level 1" or "Stir" mode. The dasher will begin to turn in the bowl. Pour the refrigerated mixture immediately from the mixing bowl into the freezer bowl.

8. After approximately 20 minutes (in the last five minutes of freezing), add the nougat pieces, the caramel chips, and the chocolate syrup into the ice cream bowl to let mix completely.

9. After approximately 25-30 minutes (total), the mixture will have frozen to a thick, creamy soft-serve consistency, with the chocolate, caramel and nougat swirled in delicious chunky ribbons. Serve directly from the ice cream freezer bowl into serving bowls or cones, and enjoy!

10. For a more hard-frozen consistency, transfer the mixture from the freezer bowl into an air-tight container and keep in the freezer for at least 2 more hours.

BLUEBERRY AND WHITE CHOCOLATE CHIP FRO-YO

If you've never tried blueberries and white chocolate together, you're in for a delicious surprise. The juicy tart berries go so perfectly with the creamy white chocolate, making this the ideal cold treat to enjoy on a warm day.

INGREDIENTS:

1 ½ cups of whole milk

1 cup of ripe blueberries, rinsed and patted dry (frozen are fine, if thawed and drained of excess liquid)

1 ½ cups of white chocolate chips

1 ½ cups of granulated sugar

3 cups of fat free vanilla yogurt

¼ cup of heavy cream

1 ½ teaspoons of vanilla extract

INSTRUCTIONS:

1. Make sure your freezer is set at or below 0 degrees Fahrenheit (-18 degrees Celsius). Place the ice cream bowl attachment in the freezer for at least 15 hours.
2. Check that the ice cream bowl is completely frozen by giving it a shake before use. If you hear no movement, the bowl's cooling liquid is properly frozen.
3. Using your stand mixer and a mixing bowl, combine the milk with the sugar until the sugar is fully dissolved.
4. Stir in the vanilla extract, the heavy cream, and the yogurt, stirring thoroughly until all ingredients are evenly combined. Cover and refrigerate for 1-2 hours.

5. Take the ice cream freezer bowl out of the freezer and set it on the middle of your stand mixer's base.

6. Slide the assembly drive onto the bottom of the mixer head. Fit the dasher into the bowl and connect to the assembly drive.

7. When your stand mixer is prepared, switch it into "Level 1" or "Stir" mode. The dasher will begin to turn in the bowl. Pour the refrigerated mixture immediately from the mixing bowl into the freezer bowl.

8. After approximately 20 minutes (in the last five minutes of freezing), add the blueberries and white chocolate chips into the ice cream bowl to let mix completely.

9. After approximately 25-30 minutes (total), the mixture will have frozen to a thick, creamy soft-serve consistency, with the blueberries and chocolate chips providing chunky sweetness in every scoop. Serve directly from the ice cream freezer bowl into serving bowls or cones, and enjoy!

10. For a more hard-frozen consistency, transfer the mixture from the freezer bowl into an air-tight container and keep in the freezer for at least 2 more hours.

GUAVA BLISS FRO-YO

Guava fruit is a natural tropical blessing, but unless you live in one of the Hawaiian Islands, you're probably not likely to see it at the local market anytime soon. Thankfully, guava juice is readily available to buy from most anywhere and it makes this frozen yogurt a seriously exotic treat.

INGREDIENTS:

1 ½ cups of whole milk

1 ½ cups of pulp free unsweetened guava juice (homemade or store bought is fine)

½ cup of granulated sugar

3 cups of fat free vanilla yogurt

¼ cup of heavy cream

1 ½ teaspoons of vanilla extract

1 whole vanilla bean

INSTRUCTIONS:

1. Make sure your freezer is set at or below 0 degrees Fahrenheit (-18 degrees Celsius). Place the ice cream bowl attachment in the freezer for at least 15 hours.

2. Check that the ice cream bowl is completely frozen by giving it a shake before use. If you hear no movement, the bowl's cooling liquid is properly frozen.

3. Using your stand mixer and a mixing bowl, combine the milk with the guava juice and sugar until the sugar is fully dissolved.

4. Using a sharp knife, split the vanilla bean down the middle lengthwise, then use the blunt end of the knife to scrape out the seeds of the bean. Add seeds to the milk and discard the pod.
5. Stir in the yogurt, heavy cream and vanilla extract. Cover and refrigerate for 1-2 hours.
6. Take the ice cream freezer bowl out of the freezer and set it on the middle of your stand mixer's base.
7. Slide the assembly drive onto the bottom of the mixer head. Fit the dasher into the bowl and connect to the assembly drive.
8. When your stand mixer is prepared, switch it into "Level 1" or "Stir" mode. The dasher will begin to turn in the bowl. Pour the refrigerated mixture immediately from the mixing bowl into the freezer bowl.
9. After approximately 25-30 minutes, the mixture will have frozen to a thick, creamy soft-serve consistency. Serve directly from the ice cream freezer bowl into serving bowls or cones, and enjoy!
10. For a more hard-frozen consistency, transfer the mixture from the freezer bowl into an air-tight container and keep in the freezer for at least 2 more hours.

APPLE-CINNAMON FRO-YO

This is a wonderful frozen yogurt to have in your freezer in the autumn time, when the flavors of apple and cinnamon are so desirable. This is the kind of fro-yo that tastes great as a snack or a dessert and is the perfect addition to apple pie.

INGREDIENTS:

1 ½ cups of whole milk

1 ½ cups of unsweetened apple juice (homemade or store bought is fine)

½ cup of granulated sugar

1 tablespoon of ground cinnamon

3 cups of fat free vanilla yogurt

¼ cup of heavy cream

1 ½ teaspoons of vanilla extract

INSTRUCTIONS:

1. Make sure your freezer is set at or below 0 degrees Fahrenheit (-18 degrees Celsius). Place the ice cream bowl attachment in the freezer for at least 15 hours.

2. Check that the ice cream bowl is completely frozen by giving it a shake before use. If you hear no movement, the bowl's cooling liquid is properly frozen.

3. Using your stand mixer and a mixing bowl, combine the milk with the apple juice, cinnamon, and sugar until the sugar is fully dissolved.

4. Stir in the yogurt, heavy cream and vanilla extract. Refrigerate for 1-2 hours.

5. Take the ice cream freezer bowl out of the freezer and set it on the middle of your stand mixer's base.

6. Slide the assembly drive onto the bottom of the mixer head. Fit the dasher into the bowl and connect to the assembly drive.

7. When your stand mixer is prepared, switch it into "Level 1" or "Stir" mode. The dasher will begin to turn in the bowl. Pour the refrigerated mixture immediately from the mixing bowl into the freezer bowl.

8. After approximately 25-30 minutes, the mixture will have frozen to a thick, creamy soft-serve consistency. Serve directly from the ice cream freezer bowl into serving bowls or cones, and enjoy!

9. For a more hard-frozen consistency, transfer the mixture from the freezer bowl into an air-tight container and keep in the freezer for at least 2 more hours.

CHAI TEA FRO-YO

There is something uniquely restorative in this traditional Indian spiced milky tea. This frozen yogurt recipe is my own frozen twist on that hot favorite. Garnish with a small sprinkle of nutmeg for a treat that both looks and tastes quite sophisticated.

INGREDIENTS:

1 ½ cups of whole milk

1 ½ cups of steeped chai tea, cooled

1 ½ cup of granulated sugar

1 tablespoon of ground nutmeg

3 cups of fat free vanilla yogurt

¼ cup of heavy cream

1 ½ teaspoons of vanilla extract

INSTRUCTIONS:

1. Make sure your freezer is set at or below 0 degrees Fahrenheit (-18 degrees Celsius). Place the ice cream bowl attachment in the freezer for at least 15 hours.

2. Check that the ice cream bowl is completely frozen by giving it a shake before use. If you hear no movement, the bowl's cooling liquid is properly frozen.

3. Using your stand mixer and a mixing bowl, combine the milk with the chai tea, nutmeg, and sugar, at a low speed until the sugar is fully dissolved in the milk.

4. Stir in the yogurt, heavy cream and vanilla extract. Refrigerate for 1-2 hours.

5. Take the ice cream freezer bowl out of the freezer and set it on the middle of your stand mixer's base.
6. Slide the assembly drive onto the bottom of the mixer head. Fit the dasher into the bowl and connect to the assembly drive.
7. When your stand mixer is prepared, switch it into "Level 1" or "Stir" mode. The dasher will begin to turn in the bowl. Pour the refrigerated mixture immediately from the mixing bowl into the freezer bowl.
8. After approximately 25-30 minutes, the mixture will have frozen to a thick, creamy soft-serve consistency. Serve directly from the ice cream freezer bowl into serving bowls or cones, and enjoy!

Grapefruit Fro-Yo

My family are all huge fans of the sweet and sour tang of grapefruit juice, so little surprise, we all love our creamy grapefruit frozen yogurt. This recipe is a snap to prepare, and a delicious healthy treat for dessert or snacking anytime.

INGREDIENTS:

1 ½ cups of whole milk

1 ½ cups of pulp-free grapefruit juice (homemade or store bought is fine)

½ cup of granulated sugar

3 cups of fat free vanilla yogurt

¼ cup of heavy cream

1 ½ teaspoons of vanilla extract

INSTRUCTIONS:

1. Make sure your freezer is set at or below 0 degrees Fahrenheit (-18 degrees Celsius). Place the ice cream bowl attachment in the freezer for at least 15 hours.

2. Check that the ice cream bowl is completely frozen by giving it a shake before use. If you hear no movement, the bowl's cooling liquid is properly frozen.

3. Using your stand mixer and a mixing bowl, combine the milk with the grapefruit juice and sugar, at a low speed until the sugar is fully dissolved.

4. Stir in the yogurt, heavy cream and vanilla extract. Cover and refrigerate for 1-2 hours.

5. Take the ice cream freezer bowl out of the freezer and set it on the middle of your stand mixer's base.
6. Slide the assembly drive onto the bottom of the mixer head. Fit the dasher into the bowl and connect to the assembly drive.
7. When your stand mixer is prepared, switch it into "Level 1" or "Stir" mode. The dasher will begin to turn in the bowl. Pour the refrigerated mixture immediately from the mixing bowl into the freezer bowl.
8. After approximately 25-30 minutes, the mixture will have frozen to a thick, creamy soft-serve consistency. Serve directly from the ice cream freezer bowl into serving bowls or cones, and enjoy!

SORBETS

Sorbets! I'll admit it, this is my favorite section of this book. Yes, I love ice cream, gelato, and frozen yogurt more than I can possibly say. But there's just something about light, flavorful sorbets that make life feel like an old-timey English summer garden party, even when it's the dead of winter here at my Stateside homestead. This section contains all the requisite classics – lemon, berry, and other citrus and fruity delights – along with some seriously fresh twists, including tarragon, avocado and a dairy-free deep chocolate sorbet that is truly divine.

Once again, being able to make these delights right in one's own kitchen not only lets the imagination run wild. It also means being able to use real, fresh ingredients, where the branded products would be stuffing in all kinds of dyes and chemicals. The home-freezer can stick to foods we trust. Example? Look no further than my all natural pink lemonade sorbet in this section, which uses delicious strawberries to create a gorgeous rosy-colored treat.

Whether you're preparing a dessert for the kids, or a palate-cleanser for a sophisticated adult dinner party, this section will have you covered. Most of these recipes require making a simple syrup on the stovetop beforehand, but full instructions are included and, don't worry, it's not tricky. I guarantee that when you taste the result, the extra effort will have been more than worth it!

MANGO LIME SORBET

This wonderful sorbet takes two classic fruit flavors, and blends them together for a frozen treat that is both wholly unique, and scrumptious. The lime and mango flavors in this sorbet go so perfectly together, it's hard to eat just one scoop. It's also quite healthy, so there's no need to turn down second helpings!

INGREDIENTS:

2 ½ pounds of mango, peeled and sliced into cubes

¾ cup of filtered water

¾ cup of white sugar

1 ½ cups of lime juice (fresh squeezed or bottled, as long as it's unsweetened)

2 tablespoons of corn syrup

INSTRUCTIONS:

1. Make sure your freezer is set at or below 0 degrees Fahrenheit (-18 degrees Celsius). Place the ice cream bowl attachment in the freezer for at least 15 hours.
2. Check that the ice cream bowl is completely frozen by giving it a shake before use. If you hear no movement, the bowl's cooling liquid is properly frozen.
3. In a large saucepan, mix the sugar and water and bring to a low boil over medium to high heat.
4. Lower the heat and continue to simmer the sugar and water, on low heat, without stirring, until the sugar has fully dissolved, about 3-5 minutes.

5. Remove from heat, transfer to a mixing bowl, and allow to cool completely. This simple syrup can be pre-made and refrigerated ahead of time when making sorbet. Refrigerate until ready to move onto next steps.
6. Place the mango cubes into a food processor or blender, and blend until completely smooth and fully pureed.
7. Pour the processed puree through a fine mesh sieve, to discard any remaining seeds and pulp.
8. Using your stand mixer and a mixing bowl, combine the mango puree with the corn syrup, lime juice, and cooled simple syrup. Stir until all ingredients are evenly combined.
9. Cover and refrigerate for at least 2 hours.
10. Take the ice cream freezer bowl out of the freezer and set it on the middle of your stand mixer's base.
11. Slide the assembly drive onto the bottom of the mixer head. Fit the dasher into the bowl and connect to the assembly drive.
12. When your stand mixer is prepared, switch it into "Level 1" or "Stir" mode. The dasher will begin to turn in the bowl. Pour the sorbet immediately from the mixing bowl into the freezer bowl.
13. After approximately 25-30 minutes, the mixture will have frozen to a thick, slushy consistency. Serve directly from the ice cream freezer bowl, and enjoy!
14. For a more hard-frozen consistency, transfer the sorbet mixture from the freezer bowl into an air-tight container and keep in the freezer for at least 2 more hours.

KIWI CITRUS SORBET

Kiwi fruit is one of my absolute favorite flavors. Its the perfect balance between sweet and tart and there's just something about the green color that puts a smile on my face. This kiwi sorbet has all that, plus a touch of citrus juice, frozen for a delicious treat that's as fun to eat as it is to make.

INGREDIENTS:

2 ½ pounds of fresh kiwi fruit, peeled and cubed
¾ cup of filtered water
¾ cup of white sugar
¾ cup of tangerine juice (or orange juice)
1 tablespoon of corn syrup

INSTRUCTIONS:

1. Make sure your freezer is set at or below 0 degrees Fahrenheit (-18 degrees Celsius). Place the ice cream bowl attachment in the freezer for at least 15 hours.
2. Check that the ice cream bowl is completely frozen by giving it a shake before use. If you hear no movement, the bowl's cooling liquid is properly frozen.
3. In a large saucepan, mix the sugar and water and bring to a low boil over medium to high heat.
4. Lower the heat and continue to simmer the sugar and water, on low heat, without stirring, until the sugar has fully dissolved, about 3-5 minutes.
5. Remove from heat, transfer to a mixing bowl, and allow to cool completely. This simple syrup can be pre-made and refrigerated

ahead of time when making sorbet. Refrigerate until ready to move onto next steps.

6. Place the kiwi cubes into a food processor or blender, and blend until completely smooth and fully pureed.

7. Pour the processed puree through a fine mesh sieve, to discard any remaining seeds and pulp.

8. Using your stand mixer and a mixing bowl, combine the puree with the corn syrup, tangerine (or orange) juice, and cooled simple syrup. Stir until all ingredients are evenly combined.

9. Cover and refrigerate for at least 2 hours.

10. Take the ice cream freezer bowl out of the freezer and set it on the middle of your stand mixer's base.

11. Slide the assembly drive onto the bottom of the mixer head. Fit the dasher into the bowl and connect to the assembly drive.

12. When your stand mixer is prepared, switch it into "Level 1" or "Stir" mode. The dasher will begin to turn in the bowl. Pour the sorbet immediately from the mixing bowl into the freezer bowl.

13. After approximately 25-30 minutes, the mixture will have frozen to a thick, slushy consistency. Serve directly from the ice cream freezer bowl, and enjoy!

14. For a more hard-frozen consistency, transfer the sorbet mixture from the freezer bowl into an air-tight container and keep in the freezer for at least 2 more hours.

Orange Carrot Apple Sorbet

This sorbet is seriously delicious and it packs an even more serious healthy boost. The vitamin rich carrot juice in this blend is perfectly sweetened by the apple and orange juice, without any added sugar and just a touch of corn syrup. This is a great frozen treat to serve up anytime. Its healthy enough for breakfast, and tasty enough for dessert!

INGREDIENTS:

1 ½ cups of rinsed and peeled carrots, patted dry, and coarsely grated

1 ½ cups of unsweetened, pulp-free orange juice (any homemade or store bought preparation will do)

1 ½ cups of unsweetened apple juice (any homemade or store bought preparation)

1 ½ cups of filtered water

3 tablespoons of light corn syrup

INSTRUCTIONS:

1. Make sure your freezer is set at or below 0 degrees Fahrenheit (-18 degrees Celsius). Place the ice cream bowl attachment in the freezer for at least 15 hours.

2. Check that the ice cream bowl is completely frozen by giving it a shake before use. If you hear no movement, the bowl's cooling liquid is properly frozen.

3. In a large saucepan, place the carrots and water, and bring to a boil over high heat.

4. Once boiling, reduce the heat to low-medium and simmer for approximately 15 minutes, until the carrots are cooked.

5. Remove from heat and allow to cool for 10-15 minutes.
6. Once cooled, strain the mixture through a mine mesh sieve, reserving both the cooking liquid and the carrots
7. Place the strained carrots into a food processor or blender, and add 1 cup of the reserved cooking liquid.
8. Cover and blend until the carrots and the liquid are completely smooth and pureed.
9. Once again, pour the processed puree through the fine mesh sieve, to discard any remaining carrot husks.
10. Using your stand mixer and a mixing bowl, combine the smoothly processed carrot puree with the remaining cooking liquid, and add in the corn syrup, apple juice, and orange juice. Stir until all ingredients are evenly combined.
11. Cover and refrigerate for at least 6 hours.
12. Take the ice cream freezer bowl out of the freezer and set it on the middle of your stand mixer's base.
13. Slide the assembly drive onto the bottom of the mixer head. Fit the dasher into the bowl and connect to the assembly drive.
14. When your stand mixer is prepared, switch it into "Level 1" or "Stir" mode. The dasher will begin to turn in the bowl. Pour the refrigerated mixture immediately from the mixing bowl into the freezer bowl.
15. After approximately 25-30 minutes, the mixture will have frozen to a thick, soft icy consistency. Serve directly from the ice cream freezer bowl, and enjoy!
16. For a more hard-frozen consistency, transfer the sorbet mixture from the freezer bowl into an air-tight container and keep in the freezer for at least 2 more hours.

COOL AND CLASSIC LEMON SORBET

What is summer without a refreshing lemon sorbet in your freezer? This sweet, simple staple is a must have in my icebox during the summer months. This frozen treat is the ideal palate cleanser or crisp frozen treat that everyone loves.

INGREDIENTS:

3 cups of filtered water

3 cups of granulated sugar

2 ¼ cups of freshly squeezed lemon juice

1 ½ tablespoons of finely diced zest of lemon

INSTRUCTIONS:

1. Make sure your freezer is set at or below 0 degrees Fahrenheit (-18 degrees Celsius). Place the ice cream bowl attachment in the freezer for at least 15 hours.

2. Check that the ice cream bowl is completely frozen by giving it a shake before use. If you hear no movement, the bowl's cooling liquid is properly frozen.

3. In a large saucepan, mix the sugar and water and bring to a low boil over medium to high heat.

4. Lower the heat and continue to simmer the sugar and water, on low heat, without stirring, until the sugar has fully dissolved, about 3-5 minutes.

5. Remove from heat and allow to cool completely. This simple syrup can be pre-made and refrigerated ahead of time when making sorbet. Refrigerate until ready to move onto next steps.

6. Add the lemon juice and zest to the cooled simple syrup, and stir to combine fully.

7. Take the ice cream freezer bowl out of the freezer and set it on the middle of your stand mixer's base.

8. Slide the assembly drive onto the bottom of the mixer head. Fit the dasher into the bowl and connect to the assembly drive.

9. When your stand mixer is prepared, switch it into "Level 1" or "Stir" mode. The dasher will begin to turn in the bowl. Pour the sorbet mixture immediately from the mixing bowl into the freezer bowl.

10. After approximately 25-30 minutes, the mixture will have frozen to a thick, soft icy consistency. Serve directly from the ice cream freezer bowl, and enjoy!

BERRY BLENDED SORBET

This blended berry sorbet is not only sweet, refreshing and delicious, it's also packed with vitamins, minerals, and antioxidants that you can only get with a heaping dose of berries. The blueberries and blackberries pack a seriously healthy punch, and the raspberries and strawberries render this sorbet a gorgeous deep purple color that will make it as good to look at as it is to eat!

INGREDIENTS:

¾ pound of fresh ripe blackberries, rinsed and patted dry

¾ pound of fresh ripe raspberries, rinsed and patted dry

¾ pound of fresh ripe blueberries, rinsed and patted dry

¾ pound of fresh ripe strawberries, rinsed and patted dry

1 cup of filtered water

1 cup of white sugar

1 tablespoon of corn syrup

INSTRUCTIONS:

1. Make sure your freezer is set at or below 0 degrees Fahrenheit (-18 degrees Celsius). Place the ice cream bowl attachment in the freezer for at least 15 hours.

2. Check that the ice cream bowl is completely frozen by giving it a shake before use. If you hear no movement, the bowl's cooling liquid is properly frozen.

3. In a large saucepan, mix the sugar and water and bring to a low boil over medium to high heat.

4. Lower the heat and continue to simmer the sugar and water, on low heat, without stirring, until the sugar has fully dissolved, about 3-5 minutes.

5. Remove from heat, transfer to a mixing bowl, and allow to cool completely. This simple syrup can be pre-made and refrigerated ahead of time when making sorbet. Refrigerate until ready to move onto next steps.

6. Place all the berries together into a food processor or blender, and blend until completely smooth and fully pureed.

7. Pour the processed puree through a fine mesh sieve and discard the seeds, skins, and pulp.

8. Using your stand mixer and a mixing bowl, combine the smoothly processed berry puree with the corn syrup and cooled simple syrup. Stir until all ingredients are evenly combined.

9. Cover and refrigerate for at least 2 hours.

10. Take the ice cream freezer bowl out of the freezer and set it on the middle of your stand mixer's base.

11. Slide the assembly drive onto the bottom of the mixer head. Fit the dasher into the bowl and connect to the assembly drive.

12. When your stand mixer is prepared, switch it into "Level 1" or "Stir" mode. The dasher will begin to turn in the bowl. Pour the refrigerated mixture immediately from the mixing bowl into the freezer bowl.

13. After approximately 25-30 minutes, the mixture will have frozen to a thick, slushy consistency. Serve directly from the ice cream freezer bowl, and enjoy!

14. For a more hard-frozen consistency, transfer the sorbet mixture from the freezer bowl into an air-tight container and keep in the freezer for at least 2 more hours.

Tropical Fandango Sorbet

Get ready for a taste of the tropics – frozen style! This awesome fruity sorbet is a perfect blend of pineapple juice, passion fruit nectar, and coconut milk. The result is a sweet and exotic flavor unlike any other. With no added sugar, this is also a wonderfully healthy choice – so go ahead and indulge, without the guilt!

INGREDIENTS:

2 ½ cups of strained unsweetened pineapple juice (canned is fine)

3 tablespoons of strained passion fruit nectar

2 cups of coconut milk

1 ½ cups of filtered water

3 tablespoons of light corn syrup

INSTRUCTIONS:

1. Make sure your freezer is set at or below 0 degrees Fahrenheit (-18 degrees Celsius). Place the ice cream bowl attachment in the freezer for at least 15 hours.
2. Check that the ice cream bowl is completely frozen by giving it a shake before use. If you hear no movement, the bowl's cooling liquid is properly frozen.
3. Using your stand mixer and a mixing bowl, combine the pineapple juice, passion fruit nectar, coconut milk, water, and corn syrup. Mix until all ingredients are evenly combined.
4. Cover and refrigerate for at least 6 hours.
5. Take the ice cream freezer bowl out of the freezer and set it on the middle of your stand mixer's base.

6. Slide the assembly drive onto the bottom of the mixer head. Fit the dasher into the bowl and connect to the assembly drive.

7. When your stand mixer is prepared, switch it into "Level 1" or "Stir" mode. The dasher will begin to turn in the bowl. Pour the refrigerated mixture immediately from the mixing bowl into the freezer bowl.

8. After approximately 25-30 minutes, the mixture will have frozen to a thick, soft icy consistency. Serve directly from the ice cream freezer bowl, and enjoy!

9. For a more hard-frozen consistency, transfer the sorbet mixture from the freezer bowl into an air-tight container and keep in the freezer for at least 2 more hours.

TARRAGON SORBET

If you think that tarragon in your spice cabinet has no use, think again. The lightly licorice-tinged flavor of tarragon is a wonderful flavor base for a sophisticated sorbet. With a touch of lemon, and perfectly sweetened and frozen, this icy treat is both delicious and unique. This is a great sorbet to serve as a palate cleanser at an elegant dinner party. Enjoy!

INGREDIENTS:

1 tablespoon of dried ground tarragon

¼ cup of unsweetened lemon juice (either fresh or bottled is fine)

1 ½ cups of filtered water

1 ½ cups of white sugar

1 tablespoon of corn syrup

INSTRUCTIONS:

1. Make sure your freezer is set at or below 0 degrees Fahrenheit (-18 degrees Celsius). Place the ice cream bowl attachment in the freezer for at least 15 hours.
2. Check that the ice cream bowl is completely frozen by giving it a shake before use. If you hear no movement, the bowl's cooling liquid is properly frozen.
3. In a large saucepan, mix the sugar and water and bring to a boil over medium to high heat.
4. Lower the heat and continue to simmer the sugar and water, on low heat, without stirring, until the sugar has fully dissolved, about 3-5 minutes.

5. Remove from heat, transfer to a mixing bowl, and allow to cool completely. This simple syrup can be pre-made and refrigerated ahead of time when making sorbet. Refrigerate until ready to move onto next steps.
6. Using your stand mixer and a mixing bowl, combine the tarragon, lemon juice, corn syrup, and cooled simple syrup. Mix until all ingredients are evenly combined.
7. Cover and refrigerate for at least 2 hours.
8. Take the ice cream freezer bowl out of the freezer and set it on the middle of your stand mixer's base.
9. Slide the assembly drive onto the bottom of the mixer head. Fit the dasher into the bowl and connect to the assembly drive.
10. When your stand mixer is prepared, switch it into "Level 1" or "Stir" mode. The dasher will begin to turn in the bowl. Pour the refrigerated mixture immediately from the mixing bowl into the freezer bowl.
11. After approximately 25-30 minutes, the mixture will have frozen to a thick, slushy consistency. Serve directly from the ice cream freezer bowl, and enjoy!
12. For a more hard-frozen consistency, transfer the sorbet mixture from the freezer bowl into an air-tight container and keep in the freezer for at least 2 more hours.

BLACK AND BLUEBERRY SORBET

The phrase "black and blue" is usually associated with a bad bruise, but this wonderful recipe flips the term on its head, with the perfect tangy and sweet combination of blackberries and blueberries in this terrific sorbet.

INGREDIENTS:

1 ½ pounds of fresh ripe blackberries, rinsed and patted dry

1 ½ pounds of fresh ripe blackberries, rinsed and patted dry

¾ cup of filtered water

¾ cup of white sugar

1 tablespoon of corn syrup

INSTRUCTIONS:

1. Make sure your freezer is set at or below 0 degrees Fahrenheit (-18 degrees Celsius). Place the ice cream bowl attachment in the freezer for at least 15 hours.
2. Check that the ice cream bowl is completely frozen by giving it a shake before use. If you hear no movement, the bowl's cooling liquid is properly frozen.
3. In a large saucepan, mix the sugar and water and bring to a boil over medium to high heat.
4. Lower the heat and continue to simmer the sugar and water, on low heat, without stirring, until the sugar has fully dissolved, about 3-5 minutes.
5. Remove from heat, transfer to a mixing bowl, and allow to cool completely. This simple syrup can be pre-made and refrigerated ahead of time when making sorbet. Refrigerate until ready to move onto next steps.

6. Place the blackberries and blueberries into a food processor or blender, and blend completely smooth and fully pureed.

7. Pour the processed puree through a fine mesh sieve and discard the skins, seeds and pulp.

8. Using your stand mixer and a mixing bowl, combine the smoothly processed black and blueberry puree with the corn syrup and cooled simple syrup. Stir until all ingredients are evenly combined.

9. Cover and refrigerate for at least 2 hours.

10. Take the ice cream freezer bowl out of the freezer and set it on the middle of your stand mixer's base.

11. Slide the assembly drive onto the bottom of the mixer head. Fit the dasher into the bowl and connect to the assembly drive.

12. When your stand mixer is prepared, switch it into "Level 1" or "Stir" mode. The dasher will begin to turn in the bowl. Pour the refrigerated sorbet mixture immediately from the mixing bowl into the freezer bowl.

13. After approximately 25-30 minutes, the mixture will have frozen to a thick, slushy consistency. Serve directly from the ice cream freezer bowl, and enjoy!

14. For a more hard-frozen consistency, transfer the sorbet mixture from the freezer bowl into an air-tight container and keep in the freezer for at least 2 more hours.

CRANBERRY GINGER SORBET

This awesome cranberry and ginger sorbet is truly a taste sensation. It is as delicious as it is unique, and thoroughly refreshing as a frozen dessert or sweet snack any time of year. These flavors will delight just about any palate, with the tangy cranberry and exotic ginger truly thrilling your taste buds.

INGREDIENTS:

4 ½ cups of fresh cranberries (without stems), rinsed and drained

1 tablespoon of fresh ginger, chopped

1 ½ cups of filtered water

2 ¼ cups of white sugar

2 ¼ cups of white cranberry juice

¼ teaspoon of salt

3 tablespoons of light corn syrup

2 teaspoons of fresh finely chopped orange zest

INSTRUCTIONS:

1. Make sure your freezer is set at or below 0 degrees Fahrenheit (-18 degrees Celsius). Place the ice cream bowl attachment in the freezer for at least 15 hours.

2. Check that the ice cream bowl is completely frozen by giving it a shake before use. If you hear no movement, the bowl's cooling liquid is properly frozen.

3. In a large saucepan, place the cranberries, chopped ginger, sugar, the white cranberry juice, and water together, and bring to a boil over high heat.

4. Once boiling, reduce the heat to low-medium and simmer for approximately 15 minutes, until the sugar has fully dissolved and most or all of the cranberries have popped their skins.

5. Remove from heat and allow to cool for 10-15 minutes.

6. Once cooled, strain the mixture through a fine mesh sieve, reserving both the cooking liquid and the cranberries.

7. Place the strained cranberries into a food processor or blender, and add 1 cup of the reserved cooking liquid.

8. Cover and blend until the cranberries and the liquid are completely smooth and pureed.

9. Once again, pour the processed puree through the fine mesh sieve, to discard any remaining seeds and pulp.

10. Using your stand mixer and a mixing bowl, combine the puree with the remaining cooking liquid, and add in the corn syrup, salt, and orange zest. Stir until all ingredients are evenly combined.

11. Cover and refrigerate for at least 6 hours.

12. Take the ice cream freezer bowl out of the freezer and set it on the middle of your stand mixer's base.

13. Slide the assembly drive onto the bottom of the mixer head. Fit the dasher into the bowl and connect to the assembly drive.

14. When your stand mixer is prepared, switch it into "Level 1" or "Stir" mode. The dasher will begin to turn in the bowl. Pour the refrigerated mixture immediately from the mixing bowl into the freezer bowl.

15. After approximately 30 minutes, the mixture will have frozen to a thick, soft icy consistency. Serve directly from the ice cream freezer bowl, and enjoy!

16. For a more hard-frozen consistency, transfer the sorbet mixture from the freezer bowl into an air-tight container and keep in the freezer for at least 2 more hours.

DAIRY FREE DARK CHOCOLATE SORBET

If you're looking for a dessert that packs all the intensity of rich, dark chocolate, without any dairy, look no further than this rocking dark chocolate sorbet. This recipe packs the perfect chocolatey punch with just the right amount of sweetness for a truly crave-worthy frozen treat.

INGREDIENTS:

4 cups of filtered water

1 ½ cup of white sugar

½ cup of brown sugar

2 cups of packed unsweetened cocoa powder

1 tablespoon of pure vanilla extract

INSTRUCTIONS:

1. Make sure your freezer is set at or below 0 degrees Fahrenheit (-18 degrees Celsius). Place the ice cream bowl attachment in the freezer for at least 15 hours.

2. Check that the ice cream bowl is completely frozen by giving it a shake before use. If you hear no movement, the bowl's cooling liquid is properly frozen.

3. In a large saucepan, combine the water with the white and brown sugars and stir over a medium heat, stirring until the sugars have dissolved completely.

4. Add the cocoa into the saucepan and raise the heat to a simmer for approximately 2 minutes, whisking continuously.

5. Remove the mixture from the heat and transfer to a medium sized mixing bowl.

6. Add in the vanilla extract, and stir thoroughly so that it is fully combined.
7. Cover and refrigerate for at least 2 hours.
8. Take the ice cream freezer bowl out of the freezer and set it on the middle of your stand mixer's base.
9. Slide the assembly drive onto the bottom of the mixer head. Fit the dasher into the bowl and connect to the assembly drive.
10. When your stand mixer is prepared, switch it into "Level 1" or "Stir" mode. The dasher will begin to turn in the bowl. Pour the sorbet mixture immediately from the mixing bowl into the freezer bowl.
11. After approximately 30 minutes, the mixture will have frozen to a thick, soft icy consistency. Serve directly from the ice cream freezer bowl, and enjoy!
12. For a more hard-frozen consistency, transfer the sorbet mixture from the freezer bowl into an air-tight container and keep in the freezer for at least 2 more hours.

Raspberry Mint Sorbet

This sorbet is an old classic for good reason. Sweet, juicy, and slightly tart raspberries are the perfect flavor base for a perfect icy sorbet, and the mint in this recipe creates just the right crispness to the taste. My family loves this perennial favorite, and I know yours will too. Garnish with a few sprigs of mint.

INGREDIENTS:

3 pounds of fresh ripe raspberries, rinsed and patted dry

¾ cup of filtered water

¾ cup of white sugar

10 bags of mint tea, steeped in 1 cup of filtered water, chilled

1 tablespoon of corn syrup

INSTRUCTIONS:

1. Make sure your freezer is set at or below 0 degrees Fahrenheit (-18 degrees Celsius). Place the ice cream bowl attachment in the freezer for at least 15 hours.

2. Check that the ice cream bowl is completely frozen by giving it a shake before use. If you hear no movement, the bowl's cooling liquid is properly frozen.

3. In a large saucepan, mix the sugar and water and bring to a low boil over medium to high heat.

4. Lower the heat and continue to simmer the sugar and water, on low heat, without stirring, until the sugar has fully dissolved, about 3-5 minutes.

5. Remove from heat, transfer to a mixing bowl, and allow to cool completely. This simple syrup can be pre-made and refrigerated ahead of time when making sorbet. Refrigerate until ready to move onto next steps.
6. Place the raspberries into a food processor or blender, and blend completely smooth and fully pureed.
7. Pour the processed puree through a fine mesh sieve and discard the skins.
8. Remove and discard the mint tea bags that were steeping, which will leave 1 cup of chilled, strong mint tea.
9. Using your stand mixer and a mixing bowl, combine the smoothly processed raspberry puree with the corn syrup, the chilled mint tea, and cooled simple syrup. Stir until all ingredients are evenly combined.
10. Cover and refrigerate for at least 2 hours.
11. Take the ice cream freezer bowl out of the freezer and set it on the middle of your stand mixer's base.
12. Slide the assembly drive onto the bottom of the mixer head. Fit the dasher into the bowl and connect to the assembly drive.
13. When your stand mixer is prepared, switch it into "Level 1" or "Stir" mode. The dasher will begin to turn in the bowl. Pour the sorbet mixture immediately from the mixing bowl into the freezer bowl.
14. After approximately 25-30 minutes, the mixture will have frozen to a thick, slushy consistency. Serve directly from the ice cream freezer bowl, and enjoy!
15. For a more hard-frozen consistency, transfer the sorbet mixture from the freezer bowl into an air-tight container and keep in the freezer for at least 2 more hours.

HONEYDEW MELON SORBET

I'm a huge fan of the nutritional and taste values of fresh melon, and nothing showcases the light, fresh sweet goodness of the melon quite like this amazing honeydew melon sorbet. This recipe calls for tangerine juice, which is my favorite preparation, though substituting orange juice will work great as well.

INGREDIENTS:

2 ½ pounds of fresh honeydew melon cubes
¾ cup of filtered water
¾ cup of white sugar
¾ cup of tangerine juice (or orange juice)
1 tablespoon of corn syrup

INSTRUCTIONS:

1. Make sure your freezer is set at or below 0 degrees Fahrenheit (-18 degrees Celsius). Place the ice cream bowl attachment in the freezer for at least 15 hours.

2. Check that the ice cream bowl is completely frozen by giving it a shake before use. If you hear no movement, the bowl's cooling liquid is properly frozen.

3. In a large saucepan, mix the sugar and water and bring to a low boil over medium to high heat.

4. Lower the heat and continue to simmer the sugar and water, on low heat, without stirring, until the sugar has fully dissolved, about 3-5 minutes.

5. Remove from heat, transfer to a mixing bowl, and allow to cool completely. This simple syrup can be pre-made and refrigerated

ahead of time when making sorbet. Refrigerate until ready to move onto next steps.

6. Place the melon cubes into a food processor or blender, and blend until completely smooth and fully pureed.

7. Using your stand mixer and a mixing bowl, combine the puree with the corn syrup, tangerine (or orange) juice, and cooled simple syrup. Mix until all ingredients are evenly combined.

8. Cover and refrigerate for at least 2 hours.

9. Take the ice cream freezer bowl out of the freezer and set it on the middle of your stand mixer's base.

10. Slide the assembly drive onto the bottom of the mixer head. Fit the dasher into the bowl and connect to the assembly drive.

11. When your stand mixer is prepared, switch it into "Level 1" or "Stir" mode. The dasher will begin to turn in the bowl. Pour the refrigerated sorbet mixture immediately from the mixing bowl into the freezer bowl.

12. After approximately 25-30 minutes, the mixture will have frozen to a thick, slushy consistency. Serve directly from the ice cream freezer bowl, and enjoy!

13. For a more hard-frozen consistency, transfer the sorbet mixture from the freezer bowl into an air-tight container and keep in the freezer for at least 2 more hours.

APPLE HONEY SORBET

Apples and honey together are one of the most nutritious and delicious snacks that nature has to offer. This sorbet is inspired by that sweet, simple duo, and if I do say so myself, it works perfectly. This sorbet works equally well as a dessert, or just a refreshing anytime pick-me-up!

INGREDIENTS:

3 pounds of medium-sweet/semi-tart apples, peeled, cored and diced

½ cup of honey (any brand or preparation – chef's choice)

¾ cup of filtered water

¾ cup of white sugar

INSTRUCTIONS:

1. Make sure your freezer is set at or below 0 degrees Fahrenheit (-18 degrees Celsius). Place the ice cream bowl attachment in the freezer for at least 15 hours.

2. Check that the ice cream bowl is completely frozen by giving it a shake before use. If you hear no movement, the bowl's cooling liquid is properly frozen.

3. In a large saucepan, mix the sugar and water and bring to a low boil over medium to high heat.

4. Lower the heat and continue to simmer the sugar and water, on low heat, without stirring, until the sugar has fully dissolved, about 3-5 minutes.

5. Remove from heat, transfer to a mixing bowl, and allow to cool completely. This simple syrup can be pre-made and refrigerated ahead of time when making sorbet. Refrigerate until ready to move onto next steps.

6. Place the apple chunks into a food processor or blender, and blend until fully pureed.
7. Pour the processed puree through a fine mesh sieve, to discard pulp.
8. Using your stand mixer and a mixing bowl, combine the smoothly processed apple puree with the honey and cooled simple syrup. Stir until all ingredients are evenly combined.
9. Cover and refrigerate for at least 2 hours.
10. Take the ice cream freezer bowl out of the freezer and set it on the middle of your stand mixer's base.
11. Slide the assembly drive onto the bottom of the mixer head. Fit the dasher into the bowl and connect to the assembly drive.
12. When your stand mixer is prepared, switch it into "Level 1" or "Stir" mode. The dasher will begin to turn in the bowl. Pour the refrigerated sorbet mixture immediately from the mixing bowl into the freezer bowl.
13. After approximately 25-30 minutes, the mixture will have frozen to a thick, slushy consistency. Serve directly from the ice cream freezer bowl, and enjoy!
14. For a more hard-frozen consistency, transfer the sorbet mixture from the freezer bowl into an air-tight container and keep in the freezer for at least 2 more hours.

All-Natural Pink Lemonade Sorbet

This luscious little recipe mixes strawberries with lemon juice for an all-natural, perfectly pink lemonade sorbet. Garnish this beautiful pink lemonade sorbet with a few extra slices of lemon and strawberry, or even a dollop of whipped cream. However you serve it, this sorbet will be a sweet treat that is as gorgeous to look at as it is scrumptious to eat.

INGREDIENTS:

3 cups of filtered water

3 cups of granulated sugar

2 ½ cups of fresh strawberries, rinsed and patted dry

2 ¼ cups of freshly squeezed lemon juice

1 ½ tablespoons of finely diced zest of lemon

INSTRUCTIONS:

1. Make sure your freezer is set at or below 0 degrees Fahrenheit (-18 degrees Celsius). Place the ice cream bowl attachment in the freezer for at least 15 hours.

2. Check that the ice cream bowl is completely frozen by giving it a shake before use. If you hear no movement, the bowl's cooling liquid is properly frozen.

3. In a food processor or blender, puree the strawberries until quite smooth, then strain the strawberry juice through a fine mesh sieve and discard the seeds and husks. Set aside the approximately 1 ½ cups of strawberry juice that will have strained through.

4. In a large saucepan, mix the sugar and water and bring to a low boil over medium to high heat.

5. Lower the heat and continue to simmer the sugar and water, on low heat, without stirring, until the sugar has fully dissolved, about 3-5 minutes.
6. Remove from heat and allow to cool completely. This simple syrup can be pre-made and refrigerated ahead of time when making sorbet. Refrigerate about 2 hours or until ready to move onto next steps.
7. Add the reserved strawberry juice, and the lemon juice and zest, to the cooled simple syrup, and stir to combine fully. Chill in the refrigerator for 1-2 hours.
8. Take the ice cream freezer bowl out of the freezer and set it on the middle of your stand mixer's base.
9. Slide the assembly drive onto the bottom of the mixer head. Fit the dasher into the bowl and connect to the assembly drive.
10. When your stand mixer is prepared, switch it into "Level 1" or "Stir" mode. The dasher will begin to turn in the bowl. Pour the refrigerated sorbet mixture immediately from the mixing bowl into the freezer bowl.
11. After approximately 30 minutes, the mixture will have frozen to a thick, soft icy consistency. Serve directly from the ice cream freezer bowl, and enjoy!
12. For a more hard-frozen consistency, transfer the sorbet mixture from the freezer bowl into an air-tight container and keep in the freezer for at least 2 more hours.

SWEET CHERRY SORBET

If you happen to find fresh ripe cherries at the market, make a dive for them and whip up this amazing sweet cherry sorbet. This recipe uses a touch of tangy lemon juice for the perfect flavor balance, creating the perfect frozen fruity treat for your friends, family, and guests. Garnish this cherry sorbet with some fresh or whipped cream, or simply a few extra cherries!

INGREDIENTS:

3 pounds of fresh ripe cherries, with the pits and stems discarded

1 cup of filtered water

1 cup of white sugar

½ cup of lemon juice (fresh squeezed or bottled, as long as it's unsweetened)

INSTRUCTIONS:

1. Make sure your freezer is set at or below 0 degrees Fahrenheit (-18 degrees Celsius). Place the ice cream bowl attachment in the freezer for at least 15 hours.

2. Check that the ice cream bowl is completely frozen by giving it a shake before use. If you hear no movement, the bowl's cooling liquid is properly frozen.

3. In a large saucepan, mix the sugar and water and bring to a low boil over medium to high heat.

4. Lower the heat and continue to simmer the sugar and water, on low heat, without stirring, until the sugar has fully dissolved, about 3-5 minutes.

5. Remove from heat, transfer to a mixing bowl, and allow to cool completely. This simple syrup can be pre-made and refrigerated ahead of time when making sorbet. Refrigerate until ready to move onto next steps.
6. Place the cherries into a food processor or blender, and blend until completely smooth and fully pureed.
7. Pour the processed puree through a fine mesh sieve and discard the skins and any pulp.
8. Using your stand mixer and a mixing bowl, combine the smoothly processed cherry puree with the lemon juice and cooled simple syrup. Stir until all ingredients are evenly combined.
9. Cover and refrigerate for at least 2 hours.
10. Take the ice cream freezer bowl out of the freezer and set it on the middle of your stand mixer's base.
11. Slide the assembly drive onto the bottom of the mixer head. Fit the dasher into the bowl and connect to the assembly drive.
12. When your stand mixer is prepared, switch it into "Level 1" or "Stir" mode. The dasher will begin to turn in the bowl. Pour the refrigerated sorbet mixture immediately from the mixing bowl into the freezer bowl.
13. After approximately 25-30 minutes, the mixture will have frozen to a thick, slushy consistency. Serve directly from the ice cream freezer bowl, and enjoy!
14. For a more hard-frozen consistency, transfer the sorbet mixture from the freezer bowl into an air-tight container and keep in the freezer for at least 2 more hours.

MASCARPONE SORBET

Ok, get ready for a dessert so decadent, so luscious, so absolutely indulgent, that it should come with a warning label. This mascarpone cheese sorbet is not so easy on the hips – but boy oh boy, is it a luscious treat for the lips! This is the perfect frozen dessert to have on hand for those special occasions when you want to serve up a luxurious treat.

INGREDIENTS:

2 pounds of whipped mascarpone cheese (sometimes sold as "Italian cream cheese")

1 ½ cups of filtered water

1 ½ cups of extra-fine white confectioners' white sugar

¾ cup of lemon juice (fresh squeezed or bottled, as long as it's unsweetened)

INSTRUCTIONS:

1. Make sure your freezer is set at or below 0 degrees Fahrenheit (-18 degrees Celsius). Place the ice cream bowl attachment in the freezer for at least 15 hours.

2. Check that the ice cream bowl is completely frozen by giving it a shake before use. If you hear no movement, the bowl's cooling liquid is properly frozen.

3. In a large saucepan, mix the sugar and water and bring to a low boil over medium to high heat.

4. Lower the heat and continue to simmer the sugar and water, on low heat, without stirring, until the sugar has fully dissolved, about 3-5 minutes.

5. Remove from heat, transfer to a mixing bowl, and allow to cool completely. This simple syrup can be pre-made and refrigerated ahead of time when making sorbet. Refrigerate until ready to move onto next steps.
6. Using your stand mixer and a mixing bowl, whip the mascarpone cheese together with the lemon juice, until fully combined and fluffy.
7. Combine the whipped mascarpone and lemon juice with the cooled simple syrup. Stir until all ingredients are evenly combined.
8. Cover and refrigerate for at least 2 hours.
9. Take the ice cream freezer bowl out of the freezer and set it on the middle of your stand mixer's base.
10. Slide the assembly drive onto the bottom of the mixer head. Fit the dasher into the bowl and connect to the assembly drive.
11. When your stand mixer is prepared, switch it into "Level 1" or "Stir" mode. The dasher will begin to turn in the bowl. Pour the refrigerated sorbet mixture immediately from the mixing bowl into the freezer bowl.
12. After approximately 25-30 minutes, the mixture will have frozen to a thick, dense, creamy consistency. Serve directly from the ice cream freezer bowl, and enjoy!
13. For a more hard-frozen consistency, transfer the sorbet mixture from the freezer bowl into an air-tight container and keep in the freezer for at least 2 more hours.

PEACH SORBET

Peaches are such a simple yet luxurious pleasure. This recipe thankfully works equally well with canned and strained peaches as it does with fresh ones – though I prefer using fresh ones simply because I've got them on hand for a prettier garnish! There's no going wrong with this simple and sweet sorbet.

INGREDIENTS:

3 pounds of fresh ripe peaches, peeled and sliced into cubes with the pits discarded

1 cup of filtered water

1 cup of white sugar

1 tablespoon of corn syrup

INSTRUCTIONS:

1. Make sure your freezer is set at or below 0 degrees Fahrenheit (-18 degrees Celsius). Place the ice cream bowl attachment in the freezer for at least 15 hours.
2. Check that the ice cream bowl is completely frozen by giving it a shake before use. If you hear no movement, the bowl's cooling liquid is properly frozen.
3. In a large saucepan, mix the sugar and water and bring to a low boil over medium to high heat.
4. Lower the heat and continue to simmer the sugar and water, on low heat, without stirring, until the sugar has fully dissolved, about 3-5 minutes.

5. Remove from heat, transfer to a mixing bowl, and allow to cool completely. This simple syrup can be pre-made and refrigerated ahead of time when making sorbet. Refrigerate until ready to move onto next steps.

6. Place the peaches into a food processor or blender, and blend completely until smooth and fully pureed.

7. Pour the processed puree through a fine mesh sieve and discard the pulp.

8. Using your stand mixer and a mixing bowl, combine the smoothly processed peach puree with the corn syrup and cooled simple syrup. Stir until all ingredients are evenly combined.

9. Cover and refrigerate for at least 2 hours.

10. Take the ice cream freezer bowl out of the freezer and set it on the middle of your stand mixer's base.

11. Slide the assembly drive onto the bottom of the mixer head. Fit the dasher into the bowl and connect to the assembly drive.

12. When your stand mixer is prepared, switch it into "Level 1" or "Stir" mode. The dasher will begin to turn in the bowl. Pour the refrigerated sorbet mixture immediately from the mixing bowl into the freezer bowl.

13. After approximately 25-30 minutes, the mixture will have frozen to a thick, slushy consistency. Serve directly from the ice cream freezer bowl, and enjoy!

14. For a more hard-frozen consistency, transfer the sorbet mixture from the freezer bowl into an air-tight container and keep in the freezer for at least 2 more hours.

AVOCADO SORBET

Avocados are the fruits of the gods and I sure do believe it when I'm enjoying this divine avocado sorbet. With a touch of lime, coconut milk, and a light, silky sweetness, this creamy (yet dairy-free!) sorbet is both unusual and delicious. This sorbet is the perfect dessert or palate cleanser to accompany any meal.

INGREDIENTS:

8 large ripe avocados, with the pits and peels discarded

½ cup of coconut milk

¼ cup of unsweetened lime juice (fresh or bottled)

¾ cup of filtered water

¾ cup of white sugar

INSTRUCTIONS:

1. Make sure your freezer is set at or below 0 degrees Fahrenheit (-18 degrees Celsius). Place the ice cream bowl attachment in the freezer for at least 15 hours.
2. Check that the ice cream bowl is completely frozen by giving it a shake before use. If you hear no movement, the bowl's cooling liquid is properly frozen.
3. In a large saucepan, mix the sugar and water and bring to a low boil over medium to high heat.
4. Lower the heat and continue to simmer the sugar and water, on low heat, without stirring, until the sugar has fully dissolved, about 3-5 minutes.

5. Remove from heat, transfer to a mixing bowl, and allow to cool completely. This simple syrup can be pre-made and refrigerated ahead of time when making sorbet. Refrigerate until ready to move onto next steps.
6. Mash, whip or blend the avocados until thoroughly smooth.
7. Using your stand mixer and a mixing bowl, combine the pureed avocados with the coconut milk, the lime juice, and cooled simple syrup. Stir until all ingredients are evenly combined and smooth.
8. Cover and refrigerate for at least 2 hours.
9. Take the ice cream freezer bowl out of the freezer and set it on the middle of your stand mixer's base.
10. Slide the assembly drive onto the bottom of the mixer head. Fit the dasher into the bowl and connect to the assembly drive.
11. When your stand mixer is prepared, switch it into "Level 1" or "Stir" mode. The dasher will begin to turn in the bowl. Pour the refrigerated sorbet mixture immediately from the mixing bowl into the freezer bowl.
12. After approximately 25-30 minutes, the mixture will have frozen to a thick, slushy consistency. Serve directly from the ice cream freezer bowl, and enjoy!
13. For a more hard-frozen consistency, transfer the sorbet mixture from the freezer bowl into an air-tight container and keep in the freezer for at least 2 more hours.

PLUM SORBET

Plums have a wonderfully simple yet rich sweetness, with just a touch of sourness in every delicious bite. That unmistakable plum flavor truly makes this plum sorbet stand out, either as a refreshing snack or a frozen dessert that's elegant and scrumptious.

INGREDIENTS:

3 pounds of fresh ripe plums, peeled and sliced into cubes with the pits discarded

1 cup of filtered water

1 cup of white sugar

1 tablespoon of corn syrup

INSTRUCTIONS:

1. Make sure your freezer is set at or below 0 degrees Fahrenheit (-18 degrees Celsius). Place the ice cream bowl attachment in the freezer for at least 15 hours.
2. Check that the ice cream bowl is completely frozen by giving it a shake before use. If you hear no movement, the bowl's cooling liquid is properly frozen.
3. In a large saucepan, mix the sugar and water and bring to a low boil over medium to high heat.
4. Lower the heat and continue to simmer the sugar and water, on low heat, without stirring, until the sugar has fully dissolved, about 3-5 minutes.
5. Remove from heat, transfer to a mixing bowl, and allow to cool completely. This simple syrup can be pre-made and refrigerated

ahead of time when making sorbet. Refrigerate until ready to move onto next steps.

6. Place the plums into a food processor or blender, and blend until completely smooth and fully pureed.
7. Pour the processed puree through a fine mesh sieve and discard the pulp.
8. Using your stand mixer and a mixing bowl, combine the smoothly processed plum puree with the corn syrup and cooled simple syrup. Stir until all ingredients are evenly combined.
9. Cover and refrigerate for at least 2 hours.
10. Take the ice cream freezer bowl out of the freezer and set it on the middle of your stand mixer's base.
11. Slide the assembly drive onto the bottom of the mixer head. Fit the dasher into the bowl and connect to the assembly drive.
12. When your stand mixer is prepared, switch it into "Level 1" or "Stir" mode. The dasher will begin to turn in the bowl. Pour the refrigerated sorbet mixture immediately from the mixing bowl into the freezer bowl.
13. After approximately 25-30 minutes, the mixture will have frozen to a thick, slushy consistency. Serve directly from the ice cream freezer bowl, and enjoy!
14. For a more hard-frozen consistency, transfer the sorbet mixture from the freezer bowl into an air-tight container and keep in the freezer for at least 2 more hours.

STRAWBERRY RHUBARB SORBET

Strawberry rhubarb pie is a marvelous dessert. The combination of aromatic rhubarb with sweet strawberries is unlike anything else and this sorbet recipe captures those amazing flavors in a perfect frozen treat. A few slices of strawberry and even a sprig of the rhubarb will be a beautiful garnish for this luscious sorbet.

INGREDIENTS:

2 pounds of fresh ripe strawberries, rinsed and patted dry, with the stems discarded

1 ½ cups of fresh rhubarb, rinsed and patted dry, finely diced

1 tablespoon of butter or margarine

1 cup of filtered water

1 cup of white sugar

1 tablespoon of corn syrup

INSTRUCTIONS:

1. Make sure your freezer is set at or below 0 degrees Fahrenheit (-18 degrees Celsius). Place the ice cream bowl attachment in the freezer for at least 15 hours.

2. Check that the ice cream bowl is completely frozen by giving it a shake before use. If you hear no movement, the bowl's cooling liquid is properly frozen.

3. In a large saucepan, mix the sugar and water and bring to a low boil over medium to high heat.

4. Lower the heat and continue to simmer the sugar and water, on low heat, without stirring, until the sugar has fully dissolved, about 3-5 minutes.

5. Remove from heat, transfer to a mixing bowl, and allow to cool completely. This simple syrup can be pre-made and refrigerated ahead of time when making sorbet. Refrigerate until ready to move onto next steps.

6. Place the strawberries into a food processor or blender, and blend until completely smooth and fully pureed.

7. Pour the processed strawberry puree through a fine mesh sieve and discard the seeds and pulp.

8. In a large saucepan, simmer the diced rhubarb in the butter or margarine over a medium heat, until the rhubarb softens and becomes aromatic.

9. Drain the butter and place the simmered rhubarb into a food processor or blender, and blend completely smooth and fully pureed.

10. Pour the processed rhubarb puree through a fine mesh sieve and discard the pulp.

11. Using your stand mixer and a mixing bowl, combine the smoothly processed strawberry puree, the rhubarb puree, the corn syrup and the cooled simple syrup. Stir until all ingredients are evenly combined.

12. Cover and refrigerate for at least 2 hours.

13. Take the ice cream freezer bowl out of the freezer and set it on the middle of your stand mixer's base.

14. Slide the assembly drive onto the bottom of the mixer head. Fit the dasher into the bowl and connect to the assembly drive.

15. When your stand mixer is prepared, switch it into "Level 1" or "Stir" mode. The dasher will begin to turn in the bowl. Pour the refrigerated sorbet mixture immediately from the mixing bowl into the freezer bowl.

16. After approximately 25-30 minutes, the mixture will have frozen to a thick, slushy consistency. Serve directly from the ice cream freezer bowl, and enjoy!

17. For a more hard-frozen consistency, transfer the sorbet mixture from the freezer bowl into an air-tight container and keep in the freezer for at least 2 more hours.

LILY CHARLES

LEMON CUSTARD SORBET

If you're looking for all the creamy sweet and sour indulgence of lemon custard, without all the calories and fat of the traditional preparation, look no further than this luscious lemon custard sorbet. It has just enough milk and cream to create a rich, custard-like consistency. This sorbet is a wonderful dessert to serve on special occasions, elegant enough for adults and tasty enough for kids!

INGREDIENTS:

1 whole vanilla bean

2 cups of filtered water

2 cups of granulated sugar

2 ¼ cups of freshly squeezed lemon juice

1 ½ tablespoons of finely diced zest of lemon

¼ cup of fat free powdered milk

1 cup of heavy cream

1 ½ teaspoon of pure vanilla extract

INSTRUCTIONS:

1. Make sure your freezer is set at or below 0 degrees Fahrenheit (-18 degrees Celsius). Place the ice cream bowl attachment in the freezer for at least 15 hours.

2. Check that the ice cream bowl is completely frozen by giving it a shake before use. If you hear no movement, the bowl's cooling liquid is properly frozen.

3. In a large saucepan, mix the sugar and water and bring to a low boil over medium to high heat.

4. Using a sharp knife, split the vanilla bean down the middle lengthwise, then use the blunt end of the knife to scrape out the seeds of the bean.

5. Stir the seeds and the bean pod into the heating sugar and water. Lower the heat and continue to simmer on low heat, without stirring, until the sugar has fully dissolved, about 3-5 minutes.

6. Extract the vanilla bean pod and discard it.

7. Remove the mixture from heat and allow to cool completely. This simple syrup can be pre-made and refrigerated ahead of time when making the sorbet. Refrigerate until ready to move onto next steps.

8. Add the lemon juice, vanilla extract, powdered milk, cream, and lemon zest to the cooled simple syrup, and stir to combine fully. Refrigerate for 1-2 hours.

9. Take the ice cream freezer bowl out of the freezer and set it on the middle of your stand mixer's base.

10. Slide the assembly drive onto the bottom of the mixer head. Fit the dasher into the bowl and connect to the assembly drive.

11. When your stand mixer is prepared, switch it into "Level 1" or "Stir" mode. The dasher will begin to turn in the bowl. Pour the refrigerated sorbet mixture immediately from the mixing bowl into the freezer bowl.

12. After approximately 30 minutes, the mixture will have frozen to a thick, soft icy consistency. Serve directly from the ice cream freezer bowl, and enjoy!

13. For a more hard-frozen consistency, transfer the sorbet mixture from the freezer bowl into an air-tight container and keep in the freezer for at least 2 more hours.

KitchenAid® Ice Cream

ADULTS ONLY

Who says that ice cream, fro-yo, and other chilled goodies are meant for kids? Not me, that's for sure. Plenty of adults love all these frozen treats as much as any kid. And you know what really makes them a kick for adults? That's right, you guessed it – alcohol or caffeine.

This section includes perennial frozen favorites, like tropical piña coladas, daiquiris, and a strawberry margarita, along with new twists on old classics, such as the decadent and irresistible frozen chocolate martini. Forget expensive coffee shops and crowded bars and discover the wonderful world of creating awesome adults-only fun right in your very own freezer!

IRISH CREAM FROZEN YOGURT

Nothing takes the edge off after a long day, or puts the spark into a festive soiree, quite like Irish cream. The silky sweet liqueur, infused with whiskey, is an alcoholic dessert all by itself. My ice cream recipe kicks it up a notch, with an extra splash of whiskey. Its my go-to treat for girl's nights with my friends, as everyone enjoys it. Serve with chocolate sauce or chocolate shavings as a garnish.

INGREDIENTS:

1 ½ cups of Irish cream (I use Bailey's, but any brand or home preparation will do)

¼ cup of Irish whiskey (I prefer Jameson)

¾ cup of granulated sugar

4 cups of fat free vanilla yogurt

¼ cup of heavy cream

1 tablespoons of pure vanilla extract

1 teaspoon of coarsely ground vanilla bean

INSTRUCTIONS:

1. Make sure your freezer is set at or below 0 degrees Fahrenheit (-18 degrees Celsius). Place the ice cream bowl attachment in the freezer for at least 15 hours.
2. Check that the ice cream bowl is completely frozen by giving it a shake before use. If you hear no movement, the bowl's cooling liquid is properly frozen.

3. Using your stand mixer and a mixing bowl, combine the Irish cream and sugar, at a low speed until the sugar is fully dissolved.

4. Stir in the whiskey, yogurt, heavy cream, vanilla extract, and ground vanilla bean. Cover and refrigerate for 1-2 hours.

5. Take the ice cream freezer bowl out of the freezer and set it on the middle of your stand mixer's base.

6. Slide the assembly drive onto the bottom of the mixer head. Fit the dasher into the bowl and connect to the assembly drive.

7. When your stand mixer is prepared, switch it into "Level 1" or "Stir" mode. The dasher will begin to turn in the bowl. Pour the refrigerated mixture immediately from the mixing bowl into the freezer bowl.

8. After approximately 25-30 minutes, the mixture will have frozen to a thick, creamy soft-serve consistency. Serve directly from the ice cream freezer bowl into serving bowls or glasses, and enjoy!

9. For a more hard-frozen consistency, transfer the mixture from the freezer bowl into an air-tight container and keep in the freezer for at least 2 more hours.

FROZEN PIÑA COLADA

Piña coladas are my favorite drink to sip when I'm lucky enough to be at a pool or the beach. Thankfully, I don't have to be anywhere near the tropics to whip up a batch of these frozen cocktails. It couldn't be easier with my ice cream maker, and something about them is just that much more delicious and fun when they're properly frozen and mixed. This recipe is a snap to prepare, and a sheer delight to consume!

INGREDIENTS:

2 ½ cups of pineapple juice, unsweetened

2 cups of coconut milk

½ cup of coconut cream

1 ½ cups of white rum

½ cup of filtered water

½ cup of white sugar

INSTRUCTIONS:

1. Make sure your freezer is set at or below 0 degrees Fahrenheit (-18 degrees Celsius). Place the ice cream bowl attachment in the freezer for at least 15 hours.

2. Check that the ice cream bowl is completely frozen by giving it a shake before use. If you hear no movement, the bowl's cooling liquid is properly frozen.

3. Using your stand mixer and a mixing bowl, combine the coconut milk, coconut cream, water and sugar until the sugar is fully dissolved and the liquids are evenly blended.

4. Add the pineapple juice and rum, and stir thoroughly, again until all ingredients are fully combined. Cover and chill for 1-2 hours.
5. Take the ice cream freezer bowl out of the freezer and set it on the middle of your stand mixer's base.
6. Slide the assembly drive onto the bottom of the mixer head. Fit the dasher into the bowl and connect to the assembly drive.
7. When your stand mixer is prepared, switch it into "Level 1" or "Stir" mode. The dasher will begin to turn in the bowl. Pour the refrigerated mixture immediately from the mixing bowl into the freezer bowl.
8. After approximately 30 minutes, the mixture will have frozen to a thick, slushy consistency. Serve directly from the ice cream freezer bowl, and enjoy!

MOCHA CREAM GELATO

This gelato is sweet, smooth, and infused with rich mocha espresso. I don't recommend this before bed, because it will definitely pep you up, but for a grown-up dessert that is rich, creamy and packed with mocha flavor, it doesn't get better than this.

INGREDIENTS:

3 ¼ cups of whole milk

5 tablespoons of instant mocha espresso powder

1 cup of white sugar

1 cup of heavy cream

8 large egg yolks (separated from the whites)

¼ cup of fat free powdered milk

INSTRUCTIONS:

1. Make sure your freezer is set at or below 0 degrees Fahrenheit (-18 degrees Celsius). Place the ice cream bowl attachment in the freezer for at least 15 hours.
2. Check that the ice cream bowl is completely frozen by giving it a shake before use. If you hear no movement, the bowl's cooling liquid is properly frozen.
3. Pour the milk into a saucepan and heat until it's at a low simmer.
4. In a medium sized bowl, pour half of the warmed milk over the mocha espresso powder, and set to steep for 30 minutes.
5. After 30 minutes, the mocha espresso should be fully dissolved in the warmed milk.

6. Pour the powdered milk into the milk that remains in the saucepan, and stir gently over a low heat.
7. Using your stand mixer and a mixing bowl, whisk the egg yolks and the sugar, until evenly combined and thickened.
8. Pour the egg and sugar mixture back into the saucepan, and thoroughly stir together with the warming milk.
9. Add the mocha-infused milk into the saucepan, and raise the heat to medium. Stir the mixture continuously with a wooden spoon, until the mixture has reached a custard-like consistency.
10. Strain the custard from the saucepan into a medium sized bowl.
11. Stir in the cream until thoroughly combined, then cover and refrigerate for at least 6 hours.
12. Take the ice cream freezer bowl out of the freezer and set it on the middle of your stand mixer's base.
13. Slide the assembly drive onto the bottom of the mixer head. Fit the dasher into the bowl and connect to the assembly drive.
14. When your stand mixer is prepared, switch it into "Level 1" or "Stir" mode. The dasher will begin to turn in the bowl. Pour the refrigerated mixture immediately from the mixing bowl into the freezer bowl.
15. After approximately 25-30 minutes, the mixture will have frozen to a thick, creamy soft-serve consistency. Serve directly from the ice cream freezer bowl into serving bowls or cones, and enjoy!
16. For a more hard-frozen consistency, transfer the mixture from the freezer bowl into an air-tight container and keep in the freezer for at least 2 more hours.

SANGRIA SLUSHIES

I am a huge fan of sangria, a sweetened red wine with brandy, triple sec, fruit juice and delicious floating fruit chunks. It is the perfect aperitif or happy-hour indulgence. Now you can prepare this indulgence in your very own kitchen with the ice cream maker and enjoy a *frozen* sangria slushie. This recipe is wonderfully easy and sweet.

INGREDIENTS:

2 cups of red table wine

1 cup of brandy

½ cup of triple sec

1 ½ cups of lemon juice (bottled or freshly squeezed, unsweetened)

1 ½ cups of orange juice (bottled or freshly squeezed, unsweetened)

1 cup of white sugar

½ cup of concentrated lemonade

½ cup of orange slices, cut into bite-sized chunks

½ cup of lemon slices, cut into bite-sized chunks

½ cup of lime slices, cut into bite-sized chunks

INSTRUCTIONS:

1. Make sure your freezer is set at or below 0 degrees Fahrenheit (-18 degrees Celsius). Place the ice cream bowl attachment in the freezer for at least 15 hours.

2. Check that the ice cream bowl is completely frozen by giving it a shake before use. If you hear no movement, the bowl's cooling liquid is properly frozen.

3. Using your stand mixer and a mixing bowl, combine the lemon juice, concentrated lemonade, orange juice, and sugar. Stir thoroughly, until the sugar is fully dissolved and all ingredients are completely blended.

4. Add the triple sec, brandy, and red wine. Again, stir thoroughly until all ingredients are thoroughly blended.

5. Take the ice cream freezer bowl out of the freezer and set it on the middle of your stand mixer's base.

6. Slide the assembly drive onto the bottom of the mixer head. Fit the dasher into the bowl and connect to the assembly drive.

7. When your stand mixer is prepared, switch it into "Level 1" or "Stir" mode. The dasher will begin to turn in the bowl. Pour the refrigerated mixture immediately from the mixing bowl into the freezer bowl.

8. After approximately 25-30 minutes (in the last five minutes of freezing), add the chunks of orange, lemon and lime into the freezer bowl to let mix completely. allow to freeze another 5 minutes.

9. After approximately 30 minutes (total), the sangria will have frozen to a thick, slushy consistency, with the fruit blended and lightly frozen perfectly throughout. Transfer from the freezer bowl into glasses or a pitcher, and enjoy!

White Russian Gelato

White Russians are one of my favorite cocktails. They already taste like a dessert, with decadent coffee liqueur and sweetened milk so this gelato recipe feels like a natural extension of the fun. This is an ideal dessert to serve at an elegant adults-only dinner party, or perhaps a sinful night with friends.

INGREDIENTS:

¾ cup of vodka, thoroughly chilled

1 cup of coffee liqueur (I use Kahlua, but any preparation or brand will do)

¾ cup of white sugar

2 cups of half and half

8 large egg yolks (separated from the whites)

¼ cup of fat free powdered milk

1 cup of heavy cream

1 ½ teaspoons of pure vanilla extract

INSTRUCTIONS:

1. Make sure your freezer is set at or below 0 degrees Fahrenheit (-18 degrees Celsius). Place the ice cream bowl attachment in the freezer for at least 15 hours.

2. Check that the ice cream bowl is completely frozen by giving it a shake before use. If you hear no movement, the bowl's cooling liquid is properly frozen.

3. In a saucepan at least 2 ½ quarts in capacity, place the sugar and 1 ¼ cups of the half and half to simmer over a medium heat. Stir continuously and, once the sugar is fully dissolved, adjust the heat to low to keep the mixture warm.

4. Using your stand mixer and a mixing bowl, whisk or whip the egg yolks for approximately 2 minutes until they're thickened.

5. While whisking the egg yolks, add in ½ cup of the hot mixture, and whisk thoroughly until all ingredients are completely combined.

6. Pour the mixture with the egg yolks into the saucepan with the rest of the half and half and sugar mixture, and raise the heat under the saucepan back up to medium.

7. Continuously stir the mixture in the saucepan with a wooden spoon, until it has thickened to a custard-like consistency.

8. Stir in the remaining half and half and the powdered milk, and continue to stir for a few more minutes.

9. Remove the saucepan from the heat and strain the mixture through a fine mesh sieve into a large mixing bowl.

10. Stir in the vanilla extract, heavy cream, the chilled vodka and the kahlua, then cover the mixing bowl and refrigerate for at least 6 hours.

11. Take the ice cream freezer bowl out of the freezer and set it on the middle of your stand mixer's base.

12. Slide the assembly drive onto the bottom of the mixer head. Fit the dasher into the bowl and connect to the assembly drive.

13. When your stand mixer is prepared, switch it into "Level 1" or "Stir" mode. The dasher will begin to turn in the bowl. Pour the refrigerated mixture immediately from the mixing bowl into the freezer bowl.

14. After approximately 30 minutes, the mixture will have frozen to a thick, creamy soft-serve consistency. Serve directly from the ice cream freezer bowl into serving bowls or cones, and enjoy!

15. For a more hard-frozen consistency, transfer the mixture from the freezer bowl into an air-tight container and keep in the freezer for at least 2 more hours.

FROZEN DAIQUIRI

Prepare this sweet frozen daiquiri recipe ahead of your next cocktail party, and I guarantee you'll have your guests dancing in no time. We've all had daiquiris made in the blender, usually with messy crushed ice, but the trouble is you have to make so many batches to accommodate guests. The bartender is always busy! The beauty of mixing them up in the ice cream maker is that you can get a large batch ready in advance and you can enjoy your party, with your own daiquiri in hand, of course!

INGREDIENTS:

2 cups of lime juice, either bottled or freshly squeezed, with no sugar added
¾ cup of filtered water
¾ cup of white sugar
2 cups of white rum

INSTRUCTIONS:

1. Make sure your freezer is set at or below 0 degrees Fahrenheit (-18 degrees Celsius). Place the ice cream bowl attachment in the freezer for at least 15 hours.
2. Check that the ice cream bowl is completely frozen by giving it a shake before use. If you hear no movement, the bowl's cooling liquid is properly frozen.
3. In a large saucepan, mix the sugar and water and bring to a low boil over medium to high heat.
4. Lower the heat and continue to simmer the sugar and water, on low heat, without stirring, until the sugar has fully dissolved, about 3-5 minutes.

5. Remove from heat, transfer to a mixing bowl, and allow to cool completely. This simple syrup can be pre-made and refrigerated ahead of time when making the daiquiris. Refrigerate at least 2 hours or until ready to move onto next steps.

6. Using your stand mixer and a mixing bowl, combine the cooled simple syrup with the lime juice and the rum. Stir until all ingredients are evenly combined.

7. Take the ice cream freezer bowl out of the freezer and set it on the middle of your stand mixer's base.

8. Slide the assembly drive onto the bottom of the mixer head. Fit the dasher into the bowl and connect to the assembly drive.

9. When your stand mixer is prepared, switch it into "Level 1" or "Stir" mode. The dasher will begin to turn in the bowl. Pour the refrigerated daiquiri mixture immediately from the mixing bowl into the freezer bowl.

10. After approximately 25-30 minutes, the daiquiris will have frozen to a thick, slushy consistency. Serve directly from the ice cream freezer bowl, and enjoy!

ITALIAN ESPRESSO ICE CREAM

With a scoop of this silky Italian espresso ice cream, you can probably skip your morning cup of coffee. Use a scoop of this instead of creamer and you'll be ready to tackle any project! This ice cream is the perfect pick me up, just be careful not to indulge in too much before bedtime.

INGREDIENTS:

1 ½ cups of whole milk

1 ¼ cups of granulated sugar

3 cups of heavy cream

1 cup of freshly brewed dark Italian espresso, fully cooled

INSTRUCTIONS:

1. Make sure your freezer is set at or below 0 degrees Fahrenheit (-18 degrees Celsius). Place the ice cream bowl attachment in the freezer for at least 15 hours.

2. Check that the ice cream bowl is completely frozen by giving it a shake before use. If you hear no movement, the bowl's cooling liquid is properly frozen.

3. Using your stand mixer and a mixing bowl, combine the milk and sugar, at a low speed until the sugar is fully dissolved in the milk.

4. Stir in the brewed and cooled espresso and the heavy cream. Stir thoroughly until all ingredients are evenly blended. Refrigerate for 1-2 hours.

5. Take the ice cream freezer bowl out of the freezer and set it on the middle of your stand mixer's base.

6. Slide the assembly drive onto the bottom of the mixer head. Fit the dasher into the bowl and connect to the assembly drive.

7. When your stand mixer is prepared, switch it into "Level 1" or "Stir" mode. The dasher will begin to turn in the bowl. Pour the refrigerated mixture immediately from the mixing bowl into the freezer bowl.

8. After approximately 25-30 minutes, the mixture will have frozen to a thick, creamy soft-serve consistency. Serve directly from the ice cream freezer bowl into serving bowls or cones, and enjoy!

9. For a more hard-frozen consistency, transfer the mixture from the freezer bowl into an air-tight container and keep in the freezer for at least 2 more hours.

"OLD FASHIONED" VANILLA WHISKEY AND NUTS

I first tried an "old fashioned" cocktail after watching Mad Men, the show in which the main character "Don Draper" is constantly slinging back the sweet whiskey-and-bitters mix. The cocktail was a little strong for my taste, but then lightening struck: what if I adapted the cocktail to work as an ice cream recipe? The result is my very own "old fashioned" ice cream with whiskey and nuts, which is mellower than the cocktail itself but has a good kick. What can I say? I'm *mad* about this alcoholic ice cream, and I hope you love it too!

INGREDIENTS:

2 tablespoons of orange bitters (I use Angostura, though any preferred preparation will do)

1 ½ cups of whisky (I use Jim Beam, but any will do fine)

2 teaspoons of orange rind

2 cups of white sugar

1 ¼ cups of whole milk

3 cups of heavy cream

1 tablespoon of pure vanilla extract

1 cup of chopped walnuts

INSTRUCTIONS:

1. Make sure your freezer is set at or below 0 degrees Fahrenheit (-18 degrees Celsius). Place the ice cream bowl attachment in the freezer for at least 15 hours.

2. Check that the ice cream bowl is completely frozen by giving it a shake before use. If you hear no movement, the bowl's cooling liquid is properly frozen.

3. In a large mixing bowl, muddle the bitters with the sugar, adding the sugar gradually until it's all used and combined.

4. Add in the whole milk, and combine until the bitters and sugar are fully dissolved in the milk.

5. Stir in the vanilla extract, the whisky, the orange rind, and the heavy cream. Stir thoroughly until all ingredients are evenly blended. Cover and chill for 1-2 hours.

6. Take the ice cream freezer bowl out of the freezer and set it on the middle of your stand mixer's base.

7. Slide the assembly drive onto the bottom of the mixer head. Fit the dasher into the bowl and connect to the assembly drive.

8. When your stand mixer is prepared, switch it into "Level 1" or "Stir" mode. The dasher will begin to turn in the bowl. Pour the refrigerated mixture immediately from the mixing bowl into the freezer bowl.

9. After approximately 25-30 minutes (in the last five minutes of freezing), pour in the chopped walnuts into the freezer bowl to let mix completely. Let freeze for another 5 minutes.

10. After approximately 30 minutes (total), the mixture will have frozen to a thick, creamy soft-serve consistency, with the walnuts swirled perfectly through the sweet whisky-infused ice cream. Serve directly from the ice cream freezer bowl into bowls or cones, and enjoy!

11. For a more hard-frozen consistency, transfer the mixture from the freezer bowl into an air-tight container and keep in the freezer for at least 2 more hours.

KitchenAid® Ice Cream

FROZEN STRAWBERRY MARGARITA

This perfect summer cocktail is the ideal refreshment for adults on a hot day. The sweet strawberries and orange liqueur are perfectly complemented by the touch of lime juice in this recipe, which is fresh and tasty enough that no ready-made mix can compare. Whip up a batch today and enjoy a strawberry-sweetened frozen buzz!

INGREDIENTS:

3 pounds of fresh strawberries, rinsed and patted dry, with the stems removed

2 cups of tequila (any brand will do)

1 ½ cups of lime juice, either freshly squeezed or bottled (as long as there's no added sugar)

1 ½ cups of honey

½ cup of orange liqueur (any kind will do – I usually use Cointreau or Triple Sec)

INSTRUCTIONS:

1. Make sure your freezer is set at or below 0 degrees Fahrenheit (-18 degrees Celsius). Place the ice cream bowl attachment in the freezer for at least 15 hours.

2. Check that the ice cream bowl is completely frozen by giving it a shake before use. If you hear no movement, the bowl's cooling liquid is properly frozen.

3. Place the strawberries into a food processor or blender, and blend until completely smooth and fully pureed.

4. Pour the processed puree through a fine mesh sieve, to discard any remaining seeds and pulp.

5. Using your stand mixer and a mixing bowl, combine the smoothly processed strawberry puree with the tequila, lime juice, honey, and orange liqueur. Stir until all ingredients are evenly combined. Cover and chill for 1-2 hours.

6. Take the ice cream freezer bowl out of the freezer and set it on the middle of your stand mixer's base.

7. Slide the assembly drive onto the bottom of the mixer head. Fit the dasher into the bowl and connect to the assembly drive.

8. When your stand mixer is prepared, switch it into "Level 1" or "Stir" mode. The dasher will begin to turn in the bowl. Pour the refrigerated mixture immediately from the mixing bowl into the freezer bowl.

9. After approximately 30 minutes, the mixture will have frozen to a thick, slushy consistency. Serve directly from the ice cream freezer bowl, and enjoy!

FROZEN CHOCOLATE MARTINI

Chilled chocolate martinis have become a trendy order at bars in the last few years. But you know what's even more fun? A *frozen* chocolate martini, prepared right in your own home and ready to go in your freezer for your next adult celebration or special-occasion dessert. This recipe is simple, decadent, and downright irresistible. Have fun!

INGREDIENTS:

¾ cup of vodka, thoroughly chilled

½ cup of crème de cacao

½ cup of chocolate liqueur

1 ½ cups of whole milk

1 ½ cups of heavy cream

1 ¾ cups of white sugar

1 1/8 cups of Dutch process chocolate cocoa

2 large eggs, whole

2 large egg yolks (separated from the whites)

INSTRUCTIONS:

1. Make sure your freezer is set at or below 0 degrees Fahrenheit (-18 degrees Celsius). Place the ice cream bowl attachment in the freezer for at least 15 hours.

2. Check that the ice cream bowl is completely frozen by giving it a shake before use. If you hear no movement, the bowl's cooling liquid is properly frozen.

3. In a large saucepan, mix the whole milk and the heavy cream and warm over a low heat.

4. Using your stand mixer and a mixing bowl,, beat or whisk the sugar, Dutch process cocoa, whole eggs and egg yolks, and continue to beat or whisk until the mixture has thickened to a mayonnaise-like consistency.

5. Reduce to a low speed, and add in one cup of the hot milk and cream mixture to the mixing bowl. Mix until evenly and smoothly blended.

6. Add the entire mixture in the mixing bowl to the saucepan, and continue to stir constantly over low heat, until the mixture has thickened to a chocolate-pudding-like consistency.

7. Remove the saucepan from the heat and transfer to a large mixing bowl. Stir thoroughly until evenly combined.

8. Cover and refrigerate for at least 2 hours, until completely cooled. Once cooled, add in the chilled vodka, and stir well.

9. Take the ice cream freezer bowl out of the freezer and set it on the middle of your stand mixer's base.

10. Slide the assembly drive onto the bottom of the mixer head. Fit the dasher into the bowl and connect to the assembly drive.

11. When your stand mixer is prepared, switch it into "Level 1" or "Stir" mode. The dasher will begin to turn in the bowl. Pour the refrigerated mixture immediately from the mixing bowl into the freezer bowl.

12. After approximately 25-30 minutes (in the last five minutes of freezing), add the crème de cacao and chocolate liqueur into the freezer bowl to let mix completely.

13. After approximately 30 minutes, the cocktail will have frozen to a dense, creamy soft-serve consistency, which the crème de cacao and chocolate liqueur blended in delicious and beautiful ribbons throughout. Serve directly from the ice cream freezer bowl into serving bowls or chilled martini glasses, and enjoy!

GIN AND JUICE FRO-YO

I considered calling this the "Snoop Dog Fro-Yo," though I figured best to keep things clear. Regardless, this sweet and sassy frozen treat is of course inspired by the timeless Snoop tune, "Gin and Juice," specifically crisp apple juice and gin-soaked apple chunks, swirled into the creamy frozen yogurt for good measure. This is the perfect dessert, snack, or aperitif to whip up on a hot day when you and your adult friends are up for a little fun. Enjoy!

INGREDIENTS:

1 ½ cups of peeled apple slices, cut to small bite-sized chunks

1 ½ cups of whole milk

1 ½ cups of gin (I use Bombay, but any brand will do)

1 cup of apple juice, no sugar added

¾ cup of granulated sugar

3 cups of fat free vanilla yogurt

¼ cup of heavy cream

INSTRUCTIONS:

1. Make sure your freezer is set at or below 0 degrees Fahrenheit (-18 degrees Celsius). Place the ice cream bowl attachment in the freezer for at least 15 hours.
2. Check that the ice cream bowl is completely frozen by giving it a shake before use. If you hear no movement, the bowl's cooling liquid is properly frozen.

3. In a large mixing bowl, place the apple chunks and pour in ¾ cup of the gin, then stir gently to ensure that the apples are fully soaked. Cover and set aside, and conserve the rest of the gin for the yogurt.

4. In a separate large mixing bowl, combine the milk with the sugar until the sugar is fully dissolved.

5. Stir in the apple juice, the remaining gin, the heavy cream, and the yogurt, stirring thoroughly until all ingredients are evenly combined.

6. Take the ice cream freezer bowl out of the freezer and set it on the middle of your stand mixer's base.

7. Slide the assembly drive onto the bottom of the mixer head. Fit the dasher into the bowl and connect to the assembly drive.

8. When your stand mixer is prepared, switch it into "Level 1" or "Stir" mode. The dasher will begin to turn in the bowl. Pour the refrigerated mixture immediately from the mixing bowl into the freezer bowl.

9. After approximately 20 minutes (in the last five minutes of freezing), add the gin-soaked apple chunks into the ice cream bowl to let mix completely.

10. After approximately 25-30 minutes (total), the mixture will have frozen to a thick, creamy soft-serve consistency, with the frozen apple chunks mixed throughout. Serve directly from the ice cream freezer bowl into glasses or bowls, and enjoy!

11. For a more hard-frozen consistency, transfer the mixture from the freezer bowl into an air-tight container and keep in the freezer for at least 2 more hours.

RUM RAISIN ICE CREAM

The rum soaked raisins give this particular ice cream its unique flavor. As the ice cream sets up in the freezer, the rum flavoring from the raisins blends into the ice cream creating a hint of rum in every bite. Be sure to plan ahead to allow for this set-up time, overnight is optimal.

INGREDIENTS:

1 cup raisins

½ cup dark rum

1 cup of sugar

6 egg yolks

2 cups heavy cream

2 cups milk

1 tablespoon vanilla extract

INSTRUCTIONS:

1. Make sure your freezer is set at or below 0 degrees Fahrenheit (-18 degrees Celsius). Place the ice cream bowl attachment in the freezer for at least 15 hours.

2. Check that the ice cream bowl is completely frozen by giving it a shake before use. If you hear no movement, the bowl's cooling liquid is properly frozen.

3. In an air-tight container, place the rum and raisins. Allow the raisins to soak over night or for up to two days. Shake or stir a few times for even distribution of the rum.

4. In a saucepan of at least 2 ½ quarts capacity, add the milk and cream and heat to barely a simmer. Remove from heat.

5. Using your stand mixer and a mixing bowl, whisk or whip the egg yolks and sugar for approximately 2 minutes until they're thickened. Add vanilla extract.

6. While whisking the egg yolks, add in 1 cup of the hot mixture, and whisk thoroughly until all ingredients are completely combined.

7. Pour the egg yolks mixture into the saucepan with the rest of the milk and heavy cream and raise the heat under the saucepan back up to medium.

8. Continuously stir the mixture in the saucepan with a wooden spoon, until it has thickened to a custard-like consistency.

9. Remove the saucepan from the heat and strain the mixture through a fine mesh sieve into a large mixing bowl. Then cover the mixing bowl and refrigerate for at least 6 hours.

10. Take the ice cream freezer bowl out of the freezer and set it on the middle of your stand mixer's base.

11. Slide the assembly drive onto the bottom of the mixer head. Fit the dasher into the bowl and connect to the assembly drive.

12. When your stand mixer is prepared, switch it into "Level 1" or "Stir" mode. The dasher will begin to turn in the bowl. Pour the refrigerated mixture immediately from the mixing bowl into the freezer bowl.

13. After approximately 20 minutes (in the last five minutes of freezing), add the rum soaked raisins and any remaining rum into the freezer bowl to let mix completely

14. After approximately 25-30 minutes, the mixture will have frozen to a thick, creamy soft-serve consistency.

15. For best flavor, transfer the mixture from the freezer bowl into an air-tight container and keep in the freezer overnight before serving.

Chocolate Stout Ice Cream

If you have a chocolate sweet tooth, and if you've ever enjoyed a stout beer like Guiness, get ready to fall head over heels in love with this stout-infused chocolate ice cream. This ice cream is flavored by thick dark beer and dark cocoa-powder, with rich sweetened cream and a touch of a vanilla. In short, it's decadent deliciousness, and you really don't need a reason to whip up a batch and enjoy a scoop or three today!

INGREDIENTS:

2 ½ cups of stout beer (I use Guinness or Sam Smith's Imperial Stout, but your favorite stout or even porter will do fine)

1 cup of unsweetened dark cocoa powder

2/3 cup of white sugar

1/2 cup of packed brown sugar

1/2 cup of whole milk

2 ½ cups of heavy cream

1 tablespoon of pure vanilla extract

INSTRUCTIONS:

1. Make sure your freezer is set at or below 0 degrees Fahrenheit (-18 degrees Celsius). Place the ice cream bowl attachment in the freezer for at least 15 hours.

2. Check that the ice cream bowl is completely frozen by giving it a shake before use. If you hear no movement, the bowl's cooling liquid is properly frozen.

3. Using your stand mixer and a mixing bowl, combine the cocoa, brown and white sugar, and stir until evenly combined.
4. Add the whole milk, and combine until the cocoa and sugars are fully dissolved in the milk.
5. Stir in the vanilla extract, the stout beer, and the heavy cream. Stir thoroughly until all ingredients are evenly blended.
6. Take the ice cream freezer bowl out of the freezer and set it on the middle of your stand mixer's base.
7. Slide the assembly drive onto the bottom of the mixer head. Fit the dasher into the bowl and connect to the assembly drive.
8. When your stand mixer is prepared, switch it into "Level 1" or "Stir" mode. The dasher will begin to turn in the bowl. Pour the mixture immediately from the mixing bowl into the freezer bowl.
9. After approximately 25-30 minutes, the mixture will have frozen to a thick, creamy soft-serve consistency. Serve directly from the ice cream freezer bowl into serving bowls or cones, and enjoy!
10. For a more hard-frozen consistency, transfer the mixture from the freezer bowl into an air-tight container and keep in the freezer for at least 2 more hours.

Made in the USA
Lexington, KY
04 December 2017